"IT'S NOT JUST WHAT YOU DO BUT HOW YOU DO IT,"

says America's master magician, Milbourne Christopher. That's why this man of many marvels has done more than just offer the finest collection of practical magic ever put in one easy-to-handle volume. He tells you how to perform each of these tricks in a manner that keeps your audience continually captivated and completely in your control as you manipulate their attention and dispel their skepticism.

Here are over 100 fabulous feats that anyone can learn and everyone from a close circle of family and friends to a packed theater will applaud. The equipment needed is kept to the minimum, the pleasure offered is raised to the very maximum. All of which makes MILBOURNE CHRISTOPHER'S MAGIC BOOK the most magical treat of them all.

"HIGHLY RECOMMENDED"—*Library Journal*

MILBOURNE CHRISTOPHER has performed his thousands of tricks to audiences in over seventy countries. He had been National President of the Society of American Magicians, and currently is head of its Occult Investigation Committee. Among his many books are *Houdini: The Untold Story* and *The Illustrated History of Magic*, the definitive work in the field.

More Magic from SIGNET

MILBOURNE CHRISTOPHER'S
MAGIC BOOK

THE MASTER MYSTIFIER

A SIGNET BOOK
NEW AMERICAN LIBRARY
TIMES MIRROR

For

Robert Harbin

brilliant performer-inventor of great stage illusions.
The Zig Zag mystery, to mention only one of his creations,
has been presented by mystifiers on five continents,
though rarely with as much wit and style

The illustrations in this book are from the author's collection. Most of the technical drawings were made by magician-artist Francis J. Rigney, who for many years
illustrated the author's feats for *Hugard's Magic Monthly.* Magician-photographer
Irving Desfor covered the author's performances at Lincoln Center, Madison
Square Garden, and Hunter College, and the vanishing elephant illusion during
"The World's Greatest Magicians" telecast. Magician-photographer Charles Reynolds attended the premiere of "Christopher's Wonders" in New York.

This is an authorized reprint of a hardcover edition published by Thomas Y.
Crowell Company. The hardcover edition was published simultaneously in Can-
ada by Fitzhenry & Whiteside Limited, Toronto.

SIGNET TRADEMARK REG. U.S. PAT. OFF. AND FOREIGN COUNTRIES
REGISTERED TRADEMARK—MARCA REGISTRADA
HECHO EN CHICAGO, U.S.A.

SIGNET, SIGNET CLASSICS, MENTOR, PLUME and MERIDIAN BOOKS
are published by The New American Library, Inc.,
1301 Avenue of the Americas, New York, New York 10019

First Signet Printing, August, 1979

1 2 3 4 5 6 7 8 9

PRINTED IN THE UNITED STATES OF AMERICA

Contents

Milbourne Christopher in The World's Greatest Magicians, *an hour of international wizardry emceed by Garry Moore, CBS-TV network, January 1, 1967.*

Christopher, Cardini, master pantomimic manipulator, and P. C. Sorcar, India's greatest illusionist, conjured on The Festival of Magic, *the first video hocus-pocus spectacular, NBC-TV network, May 27, 1957.*

Magic and Magicians

This is a book of practical magic--close-up deceptions, platform and stage conjuring, and feats of simulated ESP. Most of the tricks require no special equipment. Many can be performed with borrowed objects. All are designed to entertain. A magician, by my definition, is an entertainer who amazes an audience with mysterious feats that seem to defy explanation.

The most adept conjurers delight as much with their talk as with their tricks, as much with their manner as with their manipulations. Or they pantomime so perfectly that words are superfluous.

To achieve this finesse, practice and rehearsal are essential. Preparation is as important for a close-up demonstration as it is for a stage performance. The first trick shown should immediately attract interest; the last should generate the greatest applause. While practicing, the magician rehearses what he will say along with what he will do. He commits to memory the location of every object he will use. For instance, cards in the right-hand coat pocket, coins in the left, pen in the inside coat pocket. Then he runs through the routine again and again, until there are no awkward moves or any hesitancy on his part as to the lines he will speak.

He also tries to visualize everything that can possibly go wrong with the sequences, and works out to the best of his ability a way to turn any such misfortune to his advantage.

A tape recorder can be used during rehearsal sessions. When you hear your words played back, you may decide to deliver them with more stress, or with a pause between phrases. But don't attempt to give a performance in pantomime with your recorded talk unless you can recover from an accident better than an amateur conjurer did several years ago at a regional magic convention.

His opening trick went well. During his second feat, he dropped a billiard ball. It rolled to the footlights. He retrieved it, but by then the recorded voice was describing the third feat. Though he tried valiantly to speed up his actions, he never caught up with the pace of the canned commentary.

Above all, a magician must appear to be self-assured and not tense. Audiences reflect an entertainer's moods. If the performer is nervous, spectators will sense this and share his uneasiness. When he smiles, they smile. If he works effortlessly, they relax and enjoy being fooled.

Alexander Herrmann, "Herrmann the Great," coped with accidents as though they were planned parts of his shows. Once he dropped a wooden egg the audience had thought was a real one. It bounced on the stage. This didn't faze him; he picked it up, saying it must have been layed by a decoy duck.

George McAllister, a boyhood friend in Baltimore, was as surprised as the audience when a birdcage that should have vanished when he extended his hands, flew from his fingers, up into the air and off into the wings. He laughed and improvised, "I bet you've never before seen a birdcage disappear like that." The audience laughed with him.

Sheer luck can bring a bungled deception to a happy ending. Paul Rosini, a marvelous performer, told me what happened to him during the performance of a card trick at a party. He lost track of a selected card as he was shuffling the deck. Then the pack slipped from his grasp and fell to the floor. One card turned face-up in passage. It was the selected card, though Rosini was not aware of this until the woman who had chosen it said, "Incredible! I don't know how you found it." Rosini didn't either, but he promptly took a bow.

Magicians choose their words as carefully as lawyers or politicians. Even so, audiences sometimes misunderstand them.

"After I turn away, please count twenty cards face-down on the table," Howard Huntington told a boy in Omaha. Huntington turned his back. He was startled by an unexpected peal of laughter. The boy, he later learned, had dealt the cards with one hand over his head; *his* was the face down on the table.

John Mulholland, a conjurer of world fame, never suspected

that Alexander Woollcott, the noted critic and radio commentator, would react as he did at a party. Offering Woollcott the choice of two coins, the conjurer said, "Name one." The critic tapped the closest one. "I name it Oscar."

Years ago magicians asked for volunteers and hoped they would respond quickly. If they didn't, there was an awkward stage wait. Now there are many strategies for inducing members of the audience to leave their seats.

Tossing one end of a long rope to a man, who by his expression has been enjoying the show, I tell him to wrap the end around his hand and grip the rope firmly. By gently tugging, I can then pull my "catch" to the platform.

Or I spiral a pack of cards in its case to an attractive young woman. When she catches it, I instruct her to hold the cards above her head. "They can't see the cards at the back of the hall," I continue, "would you please stand—" She rises. "And move into the aisle." Once she is there, I continue to maneuver her down the aisle, up the steps, and onto the stage.

Horace Goldin, the illusionist, told a standing member of the audience, "Please put your left foot in front of your right . . . your right in front of your left, and keep going until you're by my side."

Will Blyth, a British conjurer, secured six or seven "volunteers" as easily as one. He batted Ping-Pong balls over the footlights. He told those who caught the balls, "You have been selected purely by chance as a committee to represent the audience. Please bring the Ping-Pong balls to the stage."

At one point in Howard Thurston's full-evening illusion show, he came down into the audience and made an unexpected production. "I try to spot a celebrity in the audience. The best participants for this feat are people who have been in the news. They don't squirm when the spotlight focuses on them." Once by a prominent man's side, Thurston would reach down the back of the spectator's coat and haul out a duck.

Harry Cecil, a comedian-magician, told me in Detroit that he preferred a man with just a wisp of a moustache as an assistant. "Anyone who has one," Cecil explained, "has taken enough kidding to be a good sport on the stage."

Understandably, magicians attempt to secure good-natured people for their feats. Sometimes, however, those who try to help are too cooperative. At the Empire Theatre in Glasgow, I deliberately held up the wrong card. I planned to change it after a volunteer had grasped it between his hands.

"Is this the card you selected?" I asked. Thinking I had made a mistake and determined not to cause me embarrassment, the affable Scot said, "Yes, it is." This was not the dramatic finish I intended, but I appreciated the man's concern.

No matter how often one performs, there are always surprises. One of my volunteers in Washington was a distinguished congressman. As requested, he tied my hands securely together with a length of rope. Before I could start the escape, he reached in my side pocket and took out the cards I had used earlier. He scanned the backs for concealed marks, felt the edges, and held the cards up to the light. "Ordinary cards," he assured the other spectators. "I just wanted to make sure."

The more spectators take part in a show, the more word-of-mouth advertising the performer later receives. Almost everyone likes to tell about the time they assisted a conjurer. I once borrowed a dollar from Hamilton Owens, then editor of the Baltimore *Sun*. I tore the bill in two pieces, gave him one to hold, along with a sealed package of mints. Then I burned the remaining portion to ashes. Sprinkling the ashes over the package of mints, I asked Owens to snap the package in half. Rolled up in the holes of the mints, he found the missing part of the dollar bill. A year later when I saw him again, he took out his wallet and removed the two pieces. "Still haven't figured this out," he said.

Reactions to magic vary. Some spectators wrinkle their brows; some shake their heads; some are noncommittal; others express their feelings vividly.

Here are three responses to one of my favorite tricks: Federal Bureau of Investigation Director J. Edgar Hoover mused and said, "I don't know whether to take you into custody, or put you on the payroll." H. L. Mencken, an editor and writer, who invariably expressed himself pungently, said, "Wow, you could cure warts!" The strangest reaction came from actress Tallulah Bankhead. She gulped and moaned, "I'm going home and vivisect my dog."

Magicians who entertain at children's parties know that youngsters, for the most part, are not as polite as adults. If an exuberant boy thinks he sees the conjurer make a false move, he may shout out, "It's in your hand," or "You put it in your pocket," or "It's up your sleeve." When these conjectures follow the disappearance of a fishbowl, even the performer has to laugh.

Horace Goldin was as ingenious in luring spectators to the stage as he was in devising and presenting his fascinating Sawing a Woman in Half.

The most disconcerting shout to many conjurers is "I've seen that before" when they have done no more than simply pick up a silk handkerchief or a piece of rope. The best tactic is to invite the child to the platform to describe the feat. The odds are that the trick he's thinking of is not the one you planned to do. If the trick described is the one you were about to perform, there are at least two alternatives: one is to thank the youngster for being such a close observer; the other and best is to use the prop to demonstrate something altogether different.

The student of magic who asks for a child to assist him should be prepared for an onslaught. I have had as many as a hundred rush down the aisles. Single out a specific youngster if you require but one. When you plan to use a large group, ask for three or four, and be sure that all who come forward are onstage before you begin the trick.

Judson Cole, a popular vaudeville monologist-magician, refused to appear at children's parties. He said they would never understand his jokes. One day an agent booked him to give a performance at a Park Avenue address for a sizable fee. Cole was to arrive there at eight o'clock in the evening and entertain for an hour.

A butler met Cole at the door, took his hat and coat, then escorted him into a luxurious playroom. Three small youngsters looked up from their blocks as he came in. "My audience?" Cole asked with a frown. The butler left and closed the door.

Sixty minutes later, the butler returned. He asked the children how they had enjoyed the performance. The oldest child said it was wonderful; the youngest was still too small to talk.

"How did you keep their interest for an hour?" I asked Cole the next day when he told me the story. "I made paper dolls, tore trees from rolled-up newspapers, told stories about giants and ogres, and we played hide and seek," he said.

Embarrassing moments? Thurston recalled an astonishing feat he once performed in Philadelphia but hoped never to repeat: "I was introducing an illusion with the words, 'You are about to see a new mystery, one you will remember as long as you live.' I pointed to a cabinet on the far side of the stage. My assistants opened the doors to show that the cabinet was empty, then whirled it around to prove that no one was concealed behind it.

A peerless showman, Houdini dramatized his challenge releases so effectively that they made the front pages of the nation's newspapers.

Howard Thurston, shown here with his Indian assistant, Chundra Bey, admitted that when he disappeared he was as startled as the audience.

"As the cabinet spun, I started toward it, and accidentally stepped on the surface of an unlatched trapdoor. I was whisked from view instantly. Getting to my feet below the stage, I heard the first burst of applause. I rushed up the inside stairs, out through the wings, and on to the stage. The applause mounted. I realized then that the eyes of the audience had been on the spinning cabinet. When they glanced back at where I had been standing, I was nowhere to be seen. They thought this was the new mystery I had announced."

Only once did Stuart Cramer lose an audience. The adept Cleveland magician was performing for tourists at an inn in Yellowstone National Park. First a few people at the back of the hall left their seats; a general exodus followed. After the show he learned that Old Faithful, the geyser, had started to spout. Word of the eruption had spread through the inn. His magic was no competition for one of nature's most spectacular wonders.

It is not likely that the reader will suddenly disappear through a trapdoor or vie for attention with a geyser. Still, the experiences of other performers can help him learn to cope with smaller problems.

Max Malini, an expert sleight-of-hand artist, took liberties during his shows that a less audacious performer would never dare attempt. After a card had been selected, remembered, and replaced, he shuffled the pack and spread it, face-down, on a table. Then blindfolded, he jabbed at the cards with a sharp knife. When he pulled up the knife, the chosen card was impaled on the tip of the blade. A Cincinnati hostess berated him. "That is a Louis Sixteenth table!" The magician shrugged. "You can tell your guests that the mark was made by Malini!"

Few amateur performers give much thought to their impromptu demonstrations. More often than not, their final trick is simply the last one that has come to their mind.

A close-up performance should be planned with as much care as a stage performance. If a performer's first feat does not capture onlookers' interest, they may not wait to see the others. Even a casual exhibition should be structured. Otherwise the same methods may be repeated, and there will be an abundance of take-a-card tricks.

Make a list of the tricks you enjoy performing extemporaneously. It will be obvious that some have more impact than others. Arrange them to build to a climax.

Your talk for intimate audiences should be on a conversational level, not loud nor bombastic. It can be funny if you are a natural comedian. It should be interesting, regardless.

Resist the temptation to perform too long. Leave your audience wanting more. An unduly long demonstration can dampen enthusiasm. Better a bright five minutes than a dull hour.

If you hope to achieve perfection, don't vary your routine. Continue presenting it for different groups until you can do the tricks almost without thinking. After you have a solid basic routine, you can add to it. Be sure that any new feat fits in the sequence and is as entertaining as the earlier ones.

Before beginning a close-up routine, clear the surface on which you intend to perform. Move a vase aside, for instance, if you think it will obstruct a spectator's view. If there is insufficient light, bring a floor lamp closer to the table. It is better to perform in a corner of the room than near a door. Anyone passing through the door might distract the spectators—and at the wrong moment.

Advance preparations for shows on platforms and stages are even more extensive. Be sure that microphones are plugged in, that the sound is not overamplified, and that there is no feedback. Check both footlights and spotlights. I once saw a conjurer perform in a green haze. A previous production in the hall had arranged for green gelatin to be placed over the spots, and green bulbs to be inserted in the footlights. Usually this particular conjurer was very funny. He wasn't in that Dracula atmosphere.

If the person who will introduce you is either taller or shorter than you are, ask him to adjust the microphone to the right height for you before he bows off. If he asks you how you would like to be introduced, suggest that he limit the introduction to a few words and your name. You can type the words on an index card before you arrive to serve as a guide for him, and hope he will not say, "Here's the magician; hold on to your pocketbooks and wallets."

If there is an orchestra, though you may not have special music, suggest that they bring you on with a lively popular tune and cover your exit with another upbeat number.

Some theatres and halls have no stairs leading from the audience to the stage. If you use volunteers, this can slow the pace of your performance, especially if the only way to reach the stage is to go through a door at the side of the platform.

Max Malini used little paraphernalia during his performances. Many of his best feats were shown with playing cards and borrowed objects.

Though obviously they were not up her sleeves, Celeste Evans, a deft deceptionist, produced cards—and birds—at her fingertips.

Arrange, if possible, to have portable steps installed. Most places have at least one set stored away backstage.

There have been times when the banquet hall in which I was to appear had a well-equipped stage, but I did not perform on it. At one affair the stage was twenty feet away from the nearest row of tables. Instead of working at that distance, I arranged to perform on the floor close to the nearest row of tables.

A Raleigh, North Carolina, auditorium offered a similar challenge—a vast open space between the first row of seats and the stage. Fortunately I arrived early and suggested that a small platform I found in a storeroom be placed eight feet away from the front row. The electricians were cooperative; they adjusted the lights to zero in on this area.

Performers in the night-club and hotel floor-show field sometimes do not seem to realize that objects must be held at least shoulder high if spectators far from the ringside are to see them.

Always stay close to your paraphernalia before it is carried onstage or to the center of the floor where you will perform. Otherwise some curious person may tamper with it—not to upset you deliberately, but to satisfy curiosity. Pack your equipment away as soon as the show is over.

Buy the best and most solidly constructed luggage you can afford. Even on airlines, baggage is carelessly handled. Pack glass and other breakable objects, covered by protective wrappings, in a small satchel that you yourself carry. If you use many pieces of equipment, pack them in several suitcases, rather than in a large trunk. It is difficult, if not impossible, to fit a trunk in a taxi. Trunks also receive rougher treatment from baggage handlers than lighter containers.

Put two labels bearing your name, your destination, and your home address on each piece of luggage. If one tag is lost in transit, the odds are that the other will remain secure.

Pack the suit in which you are to perform carefully. Should arrival at your destination be delayed, you may not have time to have the suit pressed before the show.

As a boy, I wasted much time practicing tricks that were only effective on a stage, though I performed for the most part surrounded by spectators. Later I devised routines that could be shown in hotel or night-club floor shows, with onlookers on three sides and an orchestra on a platform at the back.

Working frequently under adverse conditions, I learned how to cover my secret moves from all angles and how to present my feats without traditional conjuring tables. I either carried the

Interested in magic as a boy, film star Chester Morris fe conjuring during his coast-to-coast vaudeville appearances.

objects I used on my person, or had them readily accessible on the top of a nearby piano. I also learned that uncomplicated techniques were the most deceptive.

The tricks in this book are examples of my approach to magic. The effect of a trick on the onlooker is my principal concern. The less a performer has to worry about complicated procedures, the more he can project his personality, the more his presentation will be enjoyed.

Showmanship is far more essential than digital dexterity. A showman can turn an inconsequential trick into a mighty marvel. On the other hand, a marvelous manipulator may fail to capture and hold an audience's interest because he seems more intent on what he is doing than in winning their approval.

Showmanship is establishing immediate contact with an audience and adding dramatic appeal to produce amazement and merit applause. Showmanship is selling a trick so effectively that the disappearance of a playing card seems to be as remarkable as having an automobile vanish.

Several years ago a skillful sleight-of-hand artist devised an act that was much appreciated by less adroit conjurers. Each trick blended into the one that followed. Audiences responded to this presentation coldly. The performer seemed to be conjuring solely to himself. There were no breaks where they could applaud. Another magician who worked with a full-face mask covering his features wondered why spectators lost interest in his show. Performing with one's facial expression covered by a mask is about as appealing as conjuring with a paper bag over the head. For a few moments the mask intrigues; then the immobility of the frozen face is repelling.

Audiences applaud after a singer finishes a song or a comedian delivers the punch line of a story. Audiences also appreciate the signal that a trick is over, when a close-up conjurer brings his hands to rest and looks up. Tommy Hanlon, Jr., a hilarious comedy magician, told spectators that whenever he threw a handful of confetti into the air, they should clap. He had them practice before he presented his first trick.

Dante, a master showman, said at the beginning of his full-evening illusion production that he was too old to run to the wings and dart back and forth to acknowledge applause. When the audience responded, he would hold his hands high and say "Sim." If the applause continued, he would lower them halfway and say "Sala." If the reaction was overwhelming, he would drop his hands altogether with the word "Bim." Needless to say, there were many "Sim Sala Bims" throughout his performance.

Dante's "Backstage Illusion" was a prime-example of how clever staging can enhance a mystery. Many people, he said, thought that if they were behind him, they could detect his secrets. Therefore, he would give the whole audience that opportunity.

When the music began, he and his assistants faced the curtains at the rear of the stage. He ran a comb through his white hair as a girl held a mirror. He twirled the ends of his moustache, and stroked his beard.

The music surged into his opening number. The rear curtains opened to reveal a backdrop with a sea of painted faces. Dante addressed this audience. Meanwhile the real audience saw a box being opened, closed, then placed by the side of another one in back of which an assistant was crouching. The assistant moved behind the first box as the second was opened and closed. The second box was lowered inside the first; the assistant then crawled inside them. The real audience thought they had seen how the trick was done. Then came the surprise. The assistant produced from inside the boxes was different from the person they had seen enter them. The first man had disappeared.

When this happened even the painted audience responded, real hands came through holes in the backdrop to applaud.

Masters of the deceptive arts know that it is not enough to perform a feat so that it mystifies. The real task is to devise a novel and entertaining presentation.

Give the same trick to three capable magicians. One will tell a story as he performs it; another will show it in pantomime, with misleading actions and bits of byplay before he reaches the climax. The third may combine it with another feat, and come up with a completely unexpected climax.

I would advise the reader to see as many magicians as possible. Study how they walk out on the stage or begin a close-up routine. Take note of how they work with volunteers, and what they say as well as what they do. Analyze how they build suspense, how they manipulate the audience's interest, and how they stage their concluding feat. There is more to the ancient art of honest deception than meets the casual observer's eyes.

Who can be a magician? Almost anyone really intrigued by the art and willing to study and practice. Large hands are not necessary for legerdemain. Max Malini, a short plump man, conjured for kings and presidents; he wore size 5½ gloves.

Alexander Herrmann, a major theatrical attraction before the turn of the century, was so at ease on the stage that mishaps seemed to be marvels.

Mercedes Talma, a famous coin manipulator, also had very small hands, yet she could conceal thirty half-dollars in one of them without risking detection.

At what age should one start learning magic? I began at six and gave my first public performance at twelve. Houdini was thirteen before he mastered his first feat—making a quarter disappear. Robert-Houdin worked as a clockmaker until he was approaching forty. Bert Allerton, an outstanding close-up conjurer, had gray, receding hair before he decided it was more fun to be a magician than to earn his living as a salesman. His intimate mystifications were featured at the Pump Room in the Ambassador Hotel in Chicago.

Height and weight are unimportant. There have been midget magicians and at least one very tall deceiver who once played the role of a giant. Giovanni Belzoni towered about six feet eight inches in height and had muscles of Herculean proportions. He toured as a magician-strong man in England and Ireland early in the nineteenth century. Then the Italian adventurer sailed for Egypt and won fame as the discoverer of the tomb of Seti I in the Valley of Kings and excavator of the ancient temple at Abu Simbel.

George Braund, a popular British cabaret conjurer, stuttered until he walked out on the floor. Once in the spotlight, demonstrating his magic, he talked effortlessly and amusingly. Steve Miaco, an American, could neither hear nor speak properly. Audiences were unaware of these handicaps as they applauded his pantomimic manipulations.

Pierre Brahma, an award-winning French deceptionist, presents a precisely timed routine with jewels. He is unable to hear the music that accompanies his motions, but he can see the light system that visually cues him as to the tempo and intensity of the sound.

A one-armed sleight-of-hand specialist from Argentina has captivated audiences in North and South America with his digital dexterity.

I have in my collection a self-portrait drawn by a famous magician who was born in Germany in 1674 without hands, legs, or thighs. Matthew Buchinger held the pen with his teeth. "The Little Man of Nuremberg" played the flute, trumpet, and bagpipes, and conjured with cards, balls, and boxes.

Several show-business stars began their careers as magicians, among them Johnny Carson, Dick Cavett, and Orson Bean. Film comedian Harold Lloyd baffled his friends with thought-

Dante presented his Backstage Illusion so adroitly that until the last moment spectators were sure they knew precisely how it was done.

reading feats. Chester Morris presented a magic act in vaudeville. Cary Grant is on the board of directors of the Academy of Magical Arts. Orson Welles produced his own "Mercury Wonder Show" in California.

Young magicians gain poise and the ability to captivate audiences when they perform. They also learn how to speak effectively and to understand human motivations. Charles Dickens gave elaborate private performances, as ingeniously plotted as his novels. Rudyard Kipling, another author-conjurer, was a member of the London Magic Circle. J. B. Priestly, whose *Lost Empires* has a music-hall illusionist as a principal character, joined the Circle several years ago. More recently a member of the British royal family was inducted. Prince Charles conjured with cups and balls during his initiation ceremony.

Several eminent psychologists, among them Alfred Binet and Joseph Jastrow, found that their studies of magicians' methods enabled them to approach evaluations of perceptive ability more proficiently.

Can you believe what you see? Not always. Hold one end of a long pencil loosely between your thumb and index finger so that the pencil extends horizontally. Move your hand up and down, not at the wrist but with your arm. The pencil will appear to bend like rubber. Try this to appreciate how easily the eye can be deceived.

Have you heard an object fall in another room, then experienced difficulty in finding the source of the sound? Have you been startled by the noise of a collision in the street, then opened a door or a window and looked in the wrong direction? If so, you know how fallible the ear can be.

Try this experiment with a friend: Ask him to sit in a chair with his eyes closed. Tell him you will rattle a handful of change. The friend is to point immediately in the direction of the sound. Hold your hand a few inches about his head. Shake the loosely grasped coins. Almost invariably the friend will be far off target.

There is a classical example of touch deception. Put a pencil on the palm of your left hand. Force your right middle finger across your index finger. Touch the tips of the crossed fingers to the pencil. Shut your eyes as you roll the pencil back and forth; you will feel *two* pencils.

Magic baffles the mind even more than the senses. Here's an example. Stand facing a friend. Extend your index fingers. Hold

Mercedes Talma, wife of the great illusionist Servais Le Roy, had very small hands, yet she achieved world fame as a coin manipulator.

In the early 1900's, Joseph Zaino, a midget magician, proved that the size of a performer had nothing to do with the way his conjuring was received.

the tips three inches away from the friend's eyes. Say, "Please close your eyes, and I'll put a finger on each lid."

The moment the friend's eyes shut, put the tip of the left index finger on the lid to your right, extend your left middle finger and touch its tip to the lid to your left.

Say, "I know this sounds impossible, but if you concentrate you will feel two spirit taps on your back." Reach with your free right hand and tap twice on your friend's back. Then quickly bring the right index finger back to the position it formerly held, inches away from the right lid. Just as quickly, close your left middle finger and move your left index finger to give the impression it has just been removed from the lid to your left as you say, "Open your eyes."

This sounds complicated. It isn't, as you will find by experimentation. Most subjects turn around quickly. They think someone else tapped them.

The spectator is deceived because, as Harry Kellar once said, the magician knows more about what he is doing than the audience. You know exactly what happened, but the other person is literally and figuratively in the dark.

The more you perform, the more you will learn about how the mind is misled. You will also find that if you make what seems to you to be an obvious mistake, the audience may not notice it. Misspelled words are sometimes overlooked by experienced proofreaders. They see them but are not aware of them because they are concentrating on the meaning of a sentence. It is not likely that you noted there were nineteen words in the previous sentence. Now that I have drawn your attention to this, you will probably stop reading long enough to count them.

Though a magician misleads an audience, he takes care not to confuse himself. Platform performers with poor memories can use a simple system to be sure they give a planned show in proper sequence. If the objects to be used are laid out on a table, those for the first feat are put in front, those for the second behind them, followed by those for the third. An index card, on which the routine has been typed, can also be laid on this table. A glance at it will reveal the order of the tricks.

Similar preparations aid in the smooth running of a stage show involving much equipment and many assistants. Typed routines are posted backstage in the wings. The various pieces of paraphernalia are placed side by side, with the first to be brought out the most readily accessible.

As soon as possible after a performance has been completed,

Adelaide Herrmann, widow of Herrmann the Great, never lost her head unless this was a part of her planned presentation of a decapitation feat.

Audiences were deceived, said Harry Kellar, an outstanding American mystifier, because they knew less about what was done than the magician.

preparations for the next show should be made. When I presented an illusion production twice nightly in England, fifteen minutes after the first show was over, the equipment was ready for the one that followed.

The same procedure should be followed for close-up demonstrations. If necessary, playing cards are rearranged, and replacements are made for torn papers, empty matchbooks, and other objects.

It is always wise to have one or more spare tricks for unforeseen emergencies. Most professional performers have at least two sets of the equipment. Should the first be lost or destroyed, the second will take its place.

When I travel, I always carry one small piece of luggage myself. Should the rest of my baggage be accidentally sent to the wrong destination, I can give a two-hour performance with the objects in my attaché case.

The tricks in this book have been carefully selected. Most can be done with objects close at hand with little or no advance preparation. Don't bypass a feat because once you know how it is done you think it is too simple. The simplest tricks are often the most mystifying. Seneca the Younger, a Greek writer who saw several magicians perform early in the first century A.D., said that when he knew the secret of a trick it no longer interested him. I hope my readers will study the text not to find out how the deceptions are accomplished, but to learn how to present them effectively.

Zero Mostel and Julie Harris were Christopher's foils during a close-up sequence in Magic! Magic! Magic!, *a syndicated television special.*

Direction
and Misdirection

An audience sees and remembers what an adroit magician wishes them to see. He directs their interest with his eyes, words, and carefully planned movements. The magician can assume nothing. Unless an audience has been led to believe that a closed hand holds a coin, they will not be amazed when the hand is shown to be empty. If they are not aware that an object is green, they will not be astonished when the color changes to red.

My friend Paul Ebling illustrated this point during a demonstration of gambling techniques. He passed a pair of unprepared dice with white spots for examination. Then he announced he would shake the dice and roll a seven. The seven came up as promised. This was a far more remarkable feat than the spectators realized. Until Paul reminded them that the examined dice had been green, no one had noticed that the dice on the table were red. Their interest had been focused on the white spots.

Misdirection occurs when a magician diverts attention from the method he uses to mystify. After silently shuffling a pack of cards, for example, he speaks. The eyes of every spectator go to his face; for the moment, his hands are unobserved. Usually a magician is a step ahead of the audience. When they think a

Accidental double exposure produced this unusual photograph, taken by Irving Desfor during Christopher's Houdini *show at Lincoln Center.*

single action is taking place, the move they see may be covering another one essential to the feat. Often the actual trick—that is, the action needed to produce the illusion of magic—is over before the feat, as the audience sees it, has begun.

The tricks that follow show how direction and misdirection are used. Though the magic is varied, it is based on a single sleight.

PAPER MONEY

Tearing two four-inch squares from a newspaper, the magician crumples them into balls, then puts them down. Inviting a spectator to touch one, he picks up the selected ball with his right hand, transfers it to his left hand, then closes his fingers around it. Dropping the remaining ball into his side pocket, he takes out a coin.

"Paper," he says, directing attention to the closed left hand. "Money," he adds, glancing at the coin. He taps the closed hand with the coin. "Paper money!" He opens his hand. The paper ball has mysteriously changed into a crumpled dollar bill. He smiles as he smooths out the bill between his hands, then lets it fall to the table.

This quick trick is very effective. It can be performed at a table, on a desk, or on the palm of an onlooker's hand. Preparation is minimal. Carry a crumpled dollar and a coin—preferably a half-dollar—in the right-hand side pocket of your jacket.

Before anyone knows you intend to perform, put your hands in your side pockets. Close your right middle, ring, and little finger around the bill, then take your hands from your pockets. This is a natural action. Movement by one hand only might draw attention to it.

The trick begins when you ask for a newspaper. If one isn't available, use a page from an old magazine or a sheet from a pad. Tear out the two four-inch squares, crumple them, then put them down at least an inch apart. As soon as a spectator selects one, pick it up between your right-hand thumb and index finger and place it apparently in your left hand. I say apparently because, while carrying the paper ball, you secretly exchange it for the concealed bill with a one-hand switch.

The right thumb bending inward pushes the ball into the

Child star Mason Reese assured the audience that the card which had disappeared was not under his jacket during a Christopher trick.

hand, then brings the bill forward. As the back of the hand is toward the spectator, this move will be invisible.

The left fingers close to hide the bill the moment it touches the left palm. The left hand is raised a few inches. The magician looks at it and says, "Paper." Then he reaches with his right hand for the remaining ball. Dropping it (and the concealed ball) into his side pocket, he brings out the coin. "Money."

The tapping of the coin on the closed left hand and the words, "Paper money," seemingly change the ball into a bill. Smooth out the bill; show its back as well as its front before you let it fall to the table.

You can change the paper ball into a five, ten, or twenty dollar bill. Affluent conjurers may wish to convert it into a hundred dollar one. The feat is more appreciated in foreign countries when performed with local money.

A WORD APPEARS

The one-hand switch is employed in another feat that will puzzle guests at a party. Rip two sections from a paper cocktail napkin. Crumple them, then place them on the palm of your left hand. Ask a guest to touch one. Put it in his hand, asking him to grip it firmly. Drop the remaining ball into your side pocket and bring out a cigarette lighter. Ask him to think of his first name as he stares at the flame.

When he opens his hand and the crumpled paper, his name will appear on the paper. That is, it will if earlier you wrote it on a section of another cocktail napkin and switched this crumpled ball for the one he touched before you placed it in his hand.

If, in conversation with other guests, you discover the name of a child of the person you intend to mystify, or the name of his dog, or his boat, you can conjure up this information on the paper ball he clutches in his hand.

Do not repeat this trick for the same group at a party. Even the most astonishing feat loses impact on repetition. Having seen it before, spectators will not be surprised. Later that evening you can show it to those who did not watch during your first demonstration.

Should someone ask you how the feat was done, smile and say, "'Very deftly.'"

Christopher has made many guest appearances on the Mike Douglas show, and was the first magician to be co-host with Mike for a week.

Barbara Walters interviewed Christopher several times on the NBC-TV Today show, and is shown here during a Not for Women Only program.

BAG TO BAG

Here is a more elaborate trick based on the one-hand switch. For this you will need two paper bags, a pencil, three one-dollar bills, and four squares of paper. One of the squares is crumpled and concealed by the last three fingers of your right hand before the performance begins.

Open the paper bags, show that their interiors are empty, then place them open ends up, side by side, and six inches apart on a table behind which you stand.

Squeeze the three pieces of paper into balls; do the same with the dollar bills. Place the paper balls in front of the paper bag to your left and the wadded bills in front of the bag to your right.

Pick up one of the dollars and apparently put it into the bag to your right, but actually switch it for the extra paper ball. Let the ball drop when your hand is inside the bag, but retain the bill.

Pretend to drop a paper ball into the bag at the left, but as before, retain it and let the concealed dollar bill fall. In the same way the second dollar bill is switched for a paper ball when you put your hand into the bag to the right.

Continue in this fashion until you have deposited all the crumpled bills and paper balls in the bags. Although the audience has been led to believe that there are three dollar bills in the bag at the right and three paper balls in the bag at the left, the reverse is true.

Once again the deception has been almost completed before the trick seems to take place. You still, however, have an extra paper ball concealed in the fingers of your right hand. To dispose of it, reach in your side coat pocket for a pencil, leave the paper ball there, and bring the pencil out into view.

Tap the bag on the right with the pencil as you say, "The dollar bills." Then tap the bag on the left and say, "The paper."

"When I say 'Change,' a strange thing will happen," the magician continues. "Something so weird that I sometimes wake up in the middle of the night and wonder how it is done."

He shows his hands unmistakably empty, then lifts the bags, one with each hand. He tilts the bag at his left. The crumpled dollars roll out. He tilts the other bag. The paper balls drop from it.

You can, if you wish, present this bag-to-bag transposition with audience participation. Twist the tops of the bags after the

"Magicians," Christopher told Tom Snyder on the NBC-TV Tomorrow show, *"present their wonders solely to delight and entertain spectators."*

dollar bills and the paper balls have been deposited inside them. Give the bags to two spectators, then escort your volunteer assistants to the table.

Announce that, without touching the bags, you will present an amazing feat. Take out the pencil. Wave it toward first one bag, then toward the other. The spectator to the left is told to open his bag and tilt it. The dollars pour from it to the table. Then the spectator to the right opens the second bag and, by tilting it, brings the paper balls into view.

For children's shows, use a whistle instead of a pencil. Blow the whistle to bring about the invisible passage. Note that the magician does not tell what the climax of the trick will be. If he had said that the objects would change places, there would be no surprise at the conclusion.

You can, with practice, perform this trick with red and white Ping-Pong balls. On one occasion I used trophy cups instead of paper bags to hold the balls.

When Ping-Pong balls are used, do not attempt to switch them as the hand travels to the bag. When your hand is in the bag, let the concealed ball drop, then close your fingers around the other ball to hide it.

The feat may also be shown with two kinds of nuts—walnuts and filberts, for instance—or with cellophane-wrapped candy.

ROMANY DECEPTION

Gypsy fortune-tellers frequently bilk trusting patrons with the one-hand bill switch. A fortune-teller will tie up a client's ten or twenty dollar bill in a handkerchief with seven knots, then instruct the client to sleep with the knotted handkerchief under his or her pillow for seven nights. This, the gypsy says, will surely bring good luck.

On the morning of the eighth day, when the knots are untied, a wad of newspaper is found where the money had been. By the time the police are notified of the swindle, the fortune-teller has moved to another town. Many people, however, do not report their losses. They are too embarrassed to admit their gullibility.

To demonstrate how this Romany deception is practiced, the magician borrows a twenty dollar bill, then forms it into a ball. Holding the bill between his right thumb and index finger, he asks the spectator to drape a handkerchief over the money. As the hand is being covered, the magician switches the bill for wadded newspaper previously concealed by his curled fingers. He tells the spectator to hold the "bill" through the cloth; then he reaches into his side pocket for a rubber band, leaving the bill there as he takes out the elastic.

The rubber band is fastened around the "bill" to hold it securely. Though the magician does not touch the handkerchief again, and the spectator grips the "money" firmly, it changes into worthless paper.

The performer stresses that patrons of gypsy fortune-tellers never see their money again. He, however, is an honest deceptionist. He gives the spectator a crisp new twenty dollar bill for being such an excellent assistant.

INVISIBLE EXCHANGE

One of the strongest effects utilizing the one-hand switch is presented with two volunteers. One person is told to crumple up a ten dollar bill, then to place it on the palm of his outstretched right hand. The other does the same with a one dollar bill.

Turning to the left, the magician picks up the wadded ten dollar bill, exhibits it to the audience, then returns it to the spectators's hand, telling him to close his fingers and grasp the bill firmly. A crumpled one dollar bill has been switched for the ten in the process.

Swinging to the right, the performer reaches for the hand of the volunteer on that side and pulls the hand across until the crumpled one dollar bill is within easy reach. The dollar bill is displayed by the magician, then switched for the ten before this assistant closes his fingers around it.

Taking a coin from his side pocket, and leaving the dollar there, the performer taps the coin on each of the closed hands. This seemingly causes the bills to change places. The ten is found to be in the hand that held the one dollar bill, and the one is where the ten dollar bill had been moments before.

The expressions on the volunteers' faces invariably provoke laughter as they unfold the wrinkled money and show their surprise.

It will add to the climax if the magician asks the volunteers to stand several feet apart before they open their hands.

THE DISAPPEARING DUCKS

The vital secret moves in the preceding tricks were performed either with the back of the magician's hand turned toward the audience or under cover. Masters of direction and misdirection can, however, astound audiences when the crucial move is made openly on a stage.

For many years Harry Blackstone, Sr., presented the boldest bird-vanishing feat ever conceived. He and several assistants herded a flock of ducks into an oblong, open-ended box, labeled Duck Inn. As the last duck waddled inside, another assistant, carrying off a no longer needed prop, stumbled, and fell with a clatter at the opposite side of the stage.

Blackstone turned to see what had happened—and so did every pair of eyes in the audience. Then the magician took the box apart. The ducks had disappeared.

Had the audience not been distracted by the perfectly timed and carefully rehearsed "accident" on the far side of the stage, they would have seen the inner container of Duck Inn being yanked into the wings by a cable.

Match Magic

Tricks with matches have been popular with close-up performers for years. Folders of paper matches are readily accessible.
Because of their size, matches are easily concealed. The element
of fire adds visual appeal to many tricks. Before I describe the
matchbook magic I have devised, here are two quick tricks I
learned from others as a boy. They are as interesting to spectators today as they were when I first saw them.

THE LEAPING FLAME

Strike two matches, hold one flaming in each hand. Blow out
the match in your right hand and immediately put the charred
tip an inch below the lighted tip of the other match. The
burned-out match will then burst into flame.

*Milbourne Christopher leaves the stage to perform match magic in the
audience as a CBS-TV camera covers the action from the side.*

THE MAGNETIC MATCH

This is an intriguing intimate deception. Balancing an unlighted wooden match on the palm of his open left hand so that the head of the match extends slightly to the right, the magician briskly rubs the head of another match on his coat sleeve. He touches the head of this match to the head of the one on his palm. Nothing happens. Once more he rubs the head of the second match on his sleeve, then touches it to the first. Instantly the first match jumps high in the air and falls some distance away.

Neither friction nor reverse magnetism accounts for this surprising action. The second match must be held at the end between the right thumb and index finger. The tip of the second finger is on the small portion of the match that extends below the grip.

Each time the head of the second match is touched to the first, it is placed *beneath*, not above, the head of the first one. On the second attempt, the right-hand second finger, pressing firmly, slips past the end of the match. The match snaps and propels the other one upward.

As the attention of the onlookers has been directed by the performer to the heads of the matches, this snapping motion goes unnoticed.

HOMING MATCH

One day while idly holding an open book of paper matches, I bent the match at the left of the front row forward and down. Then I put my thumb over this match so the match could not be seen. I held the folder between my thumb—over the bent match —at the front and my fingers at the back of the cover. This is a natural way to grip an open matchbook as the right hand tears out a match.

Using this means of concealment, I worked out a trick. This is how the audience sees it:

Flipping open a matchbook folder, the magician counts the matches. Suppose there are twelve. He tears them out with a single rip, then places them on the palm of a spectator's open hand. Removing one, he tells the onlooker to close his hand over the others.

"Matches have an affinity," the magician says as he strikes the match, blows it out, then drops it on the table. "When one strays from the pack, the homing instinct is compelling."

The magician picks up the charred match. He squeezes it. It disappears.

"You were holding eleven matches," he reminds the spectator. "Count them out, one by one, and see if the wanderer has returned." The spectator finds he now has the original eleven —and the charred match that vanished.

To prepare for this deception, bend a match at the left of the front row forward and down. Close the folder, inserting the flap behind the base of the bent match. Strike the match on another matchbook. Blow the flame out quickly. Put the prepared matchbook in your left-hand side pocket.

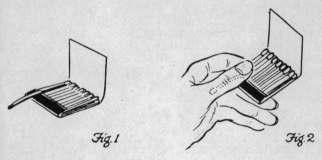

Fig. 1   *Fig. 2*

When you are ready to perform, reach for the matchbook with your left hand. While your hand is still in your pocket, grasp the bottom of the matchbook between your thumb and fingers, with the thumb over the bent match to conceal it as shown in the illustration.

Bring out the matchbook before you speak. Flip up the flap with your right hand, then fold it back so that the heads of the matches can be seen and counted.

Tear away the matches with your left hand, first bending them down over the concealed charred match. The right thumb and fingers grip the striking surface and the solid base of the matches as the tear is being made. The matches are placed on the palm of the onlooker's hand, with the charred match concealed under the others. Remove one of the upper matches, then tell the spectator to close his hand.

Strike the match, blow out the flame, then drop the match to the table about eight inches from the edge closest to you. Seem-

Queen Elizabeth and Prince Philip are amazed by the intimate conjuring of George Braund, a noted British cabaret entertainer.

ingly pick up the match with your right hand, but actually as you sweep it up, let it fall over the edge of the table. Your fingers close as though they held the match. Your eyes follow your closed hand as you raise it.

Squeeze your fingers. Open your hand. It is empty. When the spectator counts his matches, he will find the charred match he has unknowingly been gripping along with the rest.

MATCH STICKLER

In this presentation, only one match is ripped from the folder. After it has been torn away, the cover is closed, then the matchbook is held by a spectator. The match is ignited and extinguished. It disappears, then is found back in place firmly attached when the flap is opened.

As before, the bent, charred match is concealed by the thumb. After the flap has been opened, a match adjacent to the concealed one is removed. As the fingers of the right hand close the cover, the left thumb, hidden by the flap, goes under the bent match and pushes it up and back into place. While the flap is being closed, the thumb moves aside, then it presses on the top of the flap to straighten the bent match inside.

The burned match disappears as described in the previous trick. The magician takes the closed matchbook from the spectator. He opens it to show that the burned match has returned to its former position.

Pressure from the left thumb and fingertips as they hold the folder aligns the burned match with the others.

To prove that the burned match is attached, rip it away. This not only establishes this fact, but it destroys any evidence that the match has been bent.

FOUR TIMES TEN

What begins as a series of puzzles ends with unexpected magic in this tabletop diversion. The seated magician counts aloud as, one by one, he places nine matches on the table.

"Nine," he repeats. "The problem is to change nine into ten." He shows his hands both back and front; then with two matches he forms a T, with four matches makes an E, and with three constructs an N.

"I'll go a step further," he continues. "I'll change five matches into ten." Four of the nine matches are tossed aside. One of the five remaining is used for the numeral 1; the other four are arranged to make a square O.

"Now," says the magician, "to change two into ten." He throws away all but two of the matches; then he crosses one above the other to produce the Roman numeral X.

He then throws one match aside and drops the other into his left hand, closing his fingers around it immediately.

"One into ten," he announces. He squeezes his fingers, then opens his hand. It is filled with matches. He counts them rapidly. "One, two, three, four, five, six, seven, eight, nine, TEN!"

To prepare for this routine, carry nine extra matches in your otherwise empty right-hand coat pocket. The left hand does all the work in the early stages of this sequence. That is, all that the spectator sees. While the left hand throws four matches aside, then positions the remaining five to form the numeral ten, your right hand enters your side pocket and closes its fingers around the extra matches there.

TEN

Your eyes, and the spectators', are following the movements of the active left hand. You have ample time to complete this hidden maneuver as the left hand continues to attract attention, taking matches away, then putting the remaining ones in position to make first the Arabic numeral and then the Roman numeral for ten. Once you have the extra matches concealed by the curled fingers of your right hand, bring out your hand and rest it on your lap or let it hang by your side.

The moment to do this is when the X is formed. The right hand now comes into play, tossing one of the two matches in the X aside, then putting the remaining one into the left hand. The extra matches fall with it as the left hand immediately closes.

As this move is being made, the performer's eyes are not on his hands. He looks up and says, "Changing one into ten." Again the deceptive action that produces the illusion of magic has been completed before the audience realizes that the trick has started. The squeezing of the left fingers conveys the impression that a change is about to occur.

There is another finish to this routine that requires as much practice as the one just described. In this instance, the curled right-hand fingers conceal a dime. Pick up the last match, seem to put it in your left hand but retain the match and let the coin drop. The sudden conversion of a match to a ten-cent piece is even more unexpected than the appearance of ten matches.

Should you prefer to change "one into fifty," use a half-dollar instead of a dime.

UNDERCOVER OPERATION

This is one of my favorite impromptu tricks. I worked out the moves when I was in my teens and have shown it thousands of times. I have performed it for the crew of a submarine under the Atlantic Ocean and for friends in an airplane as we flew across the Pacific to Singapore. An Egyptian guide saw it as we stood on the sands of the Sahara near the Great Pyramid. He didn't applaud; he salaamed.

The magician rips the matches and striking surface out of a matchbook, then tears the cover in half. Displaying a cardboard square in each hand, he makes it clear that there is nothing concealed in his hands or under the squares. He places one square on top of the other, then lifts the top one to reveal that a large silver coin has materialized.

The half-dollar is concealed by the curled last three fingers of your right hand as you tear away the cover and divide it in two parts. As you bring the two pieces away from each other, position the coin beneath the cardboard square in your right hand, holding it in place with the tip of the middle finger, while the thumb presses from the other side. Of course, the square in your left hand is grasped in exactly the same manner. The fingers of each hand are apart. It is obvious that there is nothing concealed between your fingers or in your hands.

Bring your fingers together as you turn your left hand to the right and the right hand to the left to display the lower sides of the squares. As this is being done, the right middle finger slides the coin inward. It is hidden from view by the fingers; only a small portion of it still rests on the square.

Then, as the left hand turns to the left and the right hand turns to the right, the right middle finger slides the coin back to its previous position under the square.

Actor Edward Arnold reacts to a Christopher trick. Arnold assisted during a performance at 21, the Manhattan restaurant.

This is a very deceptive sleight. Practice and perfect it before you try the next phase of the trick. It has many uses. For example, you can conceal a silver dollar under a playing card, show the card on both sides, then place the card on a table. When you lift the card, the silver dollar mysteriously appears beneath it.

After showing both sides of the cardboard squares, you can put the square in your right hand on the one in your left hand, then remove the upper piece to disclose the coin resting on the lower square. I prefer, however, to proceed in this way: I bring my hands together, so that the square in my right hand slightly overlaps the one in my left hand. As soon as they touch, I slide across the coin with the tip of my right middle finger until the tip of the left middle finger can pull it under the left square.

I turn the right square lower side up and place it slightly overlapping the edge of the left square. As the two touch, I slide the coin with my left middle finger back under the right square, then immediately turn the left square lower side up. Then I put the right square over the left square. This brings the concealed coin between the two. I ask a spectator to tap the upper surface; I lift it, and the coin appears.

Though these instructions may appear to be complicated, if you start following them with the cardboard squares and the coin in your hands, you will find that the handling will be quite simple.

A half-dollar is the best American coin to use. Coins of approximately the same size are available in most other countries.

FLAME TO SILK

Few match tricks are as colorful as this one. The magician takes a matchbook from his pocket, tears out a match, then strikes it on the cover. Holding the burning match between the tips of his thumb and index finger, with a flick of his wrist, he converts the flame into a billowing silk handkerchief.

To prepare for this feat, twirl a sixteen-inch square of silk by the diagonal ends to reduce the circumference of the center portion. Fold the handkerchief in two-inch pleats until you are five inches from the far end. Wrap this end tightly around the bundle of compressed silk, then tuck in a portion to keep the bundle from expanding. The inch-long extending corner is inserted behind the match at the extreme right of the front row in

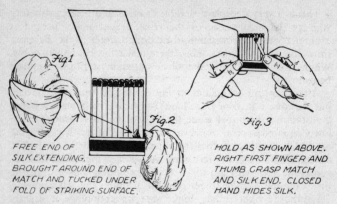

FREE END OF
SILK EXTENDING,
BROUGHT AROUND END OF
MATCH AND TUCKED UNDER
FOLD OF STRIKING SURFACE.

HOLD AS SHOWN ABOVE.
RIGHT FIRST FINGER AND
THUMB GRASP MATCH
AND SILK END. CLOSED
HAND HIDES SILK.

the folder. The corner is brought forward between this match and the one next to it, then tucked down to the right behind the upper section of the striking surface. The cover is closed. The matchbook with the bundle of silk attached to it is put in the right-hand trouser pocket.

Before you perform, curl the last three fingers of your right hand around the bundled silk and take out the matchbook at the lower right corner between the tips of your thumb and index finger. From the front it should appear that you merely removed a packet of matches from your pocket. The silk is concealed by your closed fingers. The folder, pressed between thumb and index finger, is in the position one would naturally hold it.

Bring your hands together. Open the flap with your left fingers, then use them to grip the left end of the striking surface.

The tip of the right index finger bends the last match to the right of the front row forward, then slides behind the match so that the corner of the silk at its base can be carried along with the match as the right thumb and index finger tear the match away.

It should appear that you have simply ripped out a match; your curled fingers conceal the bundle of silk. Pressing the corner of the silk to the end of the match between thumb and index finger, strike the match on the folder.

Attention is centered on the resulting flame. With a quick snap of your right wrist, release the bundled silk. It will open and expand into view. As the silk appears, the right hand turns downward, hiding the match behind the corner of the handkerchief it grasps.

Though there are no complicated moves, this production requires considerable practice. The illustrations show how the bundled silk is attached to the match, and the position of the hand as it tears the match from the folder. The thinner the silk used, the larger may be the handkerchief you produce.

How, you may wonder, do you dispose of the burned match? It can be rolled up in the silk before you tuck the handkerchief into your pocket. If you plan to use the silk for another trick, let the match drop to the floor after you have displayed the handkerchief. The trick is over as far as the audience is concerned when the silk appears. Their eyes will be fixed on your face.

TWO ON A MATCH

Two people accept cigarettes from the magician's pack. He strikes a match, then looks from one person to the other as though he has not decided which cigarette to light first. He solves the problem by producing a second lighted match.

Some performers use their thumbnails to cut the end of a paper match so that, after they have lighted it, they can pull it apart and have a lighted split section in each hand. It is better, however, to prepare the entire front row of a matchbook beforehand.

Bend a row of matches forward as shown in the illustration. Use a razor blade or a sharp knife to make the quarter-inch cut. Force the row back into its original position. This advance preparation cannot be seen when the folder is opened.

Tear out a match, strike it. When you wish to turn one match into two, bring your hands together, grip one portion of the slit between the thumb and index finger of each hand, then quickly peel the match apart. Each portion will have a flame at the far end.

A STRIKING TRICK

While you are preparing a matchbook for the divided-flame stunt, you can prepare another one for this unusual and puzzling feat devised by my friend Hen Fetsch.

Tearing two matches from a folder, the magician recalls that while on a camping trip, he found two paper matches in his duffel bag, but no striking surface. Remembering that Indians produced fire by rubbing two sticks together, he thought he would try to do so. He stroked one paper match with the other, and in seconds both burst into flame.

To do this trick, you must cut the striking surface from a matchbook into small narrow strips. Bend the front row of matches in another folder forward, then glue an oblong piece of this striking material to the back of each match, just below the head. Push the row back as it was originally, then close the flap.

When you present the feat, tear a prepared match from the front row, then one from the back row. Hold a match in each hand, with the prepared side of the first match down. When you rub the matches together, put the striking surface over the unprepared match. The lower match ignites when its head is pulled across the striking surface. The flame sets fire to the head of the upper match.

Let both burn until the matches are reduced to ashes, and no clue to the mystery is left behind.

INEXPENSIVE LIGHTER

When someone asks you for a light, reach in your pocket and bring out a matchbook—with a flaming match extending from it.

To prepare for this spectacular flourish, open a folder, bend one match forward and down until the head rests on the striking surface. Close the folder behind the bent match and put the folder in your side pocket.

When you reach for the matchbook in your pocket, close your fingers around the back and put your thumb on the match head. Press firmly to the left, scraping the head on the striking surface as you bring the folder from your pocket. This action ignites the match.

Before you try this with the matchbook in your pocket, be sure you can light the match by thumb pressure. Move your thumb aside as the fire flares up, and you will not be burned.

THE HEAVY MATCH

One night in Baltimore many years ago, Hen Fetsch and I talked about new ways to mystify with matches. He showed me how he could always tell from among several closed folders which matchbook had just been used to light a cigarette. I devised the following presentation.

The magician offers a spectator a choice of five closed matchbooks, each with a different design on the cover. While the performer's back is turned, the spectator is to tear a match from any one of the folders, close the flap, put the folder back with the others, then change their positions on the table.

The magician says he has developed an uncanny ability to sense any change in weight. He picks up the closed matchbooks, one by one, and weighs them on the palm of his hand. One, he says, is lighter than the others. Therefore, that must be the folder from which the match was taken. It is.

The matchbooks are prepared in a way that will not be suspected. Hold the bottom of an open folder firmly between the right thumb and fingers. With the thumb and index finger of the left hand, grip the flap at one side and pull it at an angle. Tug until the flap is twisted slightly to the left.

Prepare the other matchbooks in the same way. Close the flaps, aligning their sides with the striking fold, then push the flaps in securely. When someone opens one of these matchbooks and closes it, the flap will extend slightly to one side of the striking fold.

Sight, not skill in estimating weight, is the secret of this deception. When you hold each folder on your hand, look for the telltale extension.

Experiment with many folders. Some are better for this feat than others. Be sure the flaps are pressed in firmly before you begin the presentation.

When the trick is over, gather up the matchbooks casually and put them away. If they remained on the table, the spectator might examine them closely. Why risk detection?

A trick with a handkerchief was in the opening scene of Christopher's Wonders, a full-evening show that opened in New York City in 1960.

Handkerchief Hocus-Pocus

Only a few centuries ago in Cologne, a girl was charged with practicing witchcraft for tearing a handkerchief into shreds, then mysteriously restoring it. Legerdemain which the authorities did not understand was thought to have been accomplished by satanic means. In those days a proficient magician risked being jailed or burned at the stake.

Modern audiences are more tolerant—fortunately for modern magicians. Even the few spectators who still believe that conjurers, despite their disavowals of occult powers, actually have them, do not suggest that they be pilloried, or tortured. Therefore, the feat I am about to describe may be performed without trepidation today, though it would have provoked cries of terror and swift incarceration in medieval Europe.

UP IN FLAMES

"After years of experimentation," the magician begins, "I have developed a perfect fireproofing solution. A few drops of this powerful liquid on any fabric, and it will withstand high-intensity flames."

He removes his pocket handkerchief, and grasps it with his left hand so that a six-inch portion of the center extends above his closed fingers.

"This is the first public demonstration," he continues, as he saturates the cloth. He lights a match, brings it near the wet material, then pulls his hand away.

"Please note that this test takes place in full view."

He moves the match toward the handkerchief again. The cloth catches fire. A ten-inch-high blast of flame shoots up.

Responding quickly, the distressed performer beats the handkerchief and snuffs out the fire with his hands.

Attempting to smile, he says, "My next trick—." Then, remembering he is a magician, he sets about to repair the damage by making a dramatic gesture over the wadded cloth. Holding out the handkerchief between his hands, he shows the expected hole is not at its center. There is not even the slightest reminder of the incineration.

An advertisement in a conjuring journal would proclaim that this incredible feat is accomplished without substitution, that a borrowed handkerchief can be used, and that no special apparatus is required. All true!

The method was suggested by a handwritten note in a Houdini scrapbook. He said that Adrian Plate, a New York magician, poured brandy over a dollar bill in a plate, set the bill aflame, then returned it undamaged. I tried this. It worked. Then I found a handkerchief could replace the dollar bill; and cigarette-lighter fuel, the brandy. Next I worked out the fireproofing presentation.

Transfer lighter fuel from a can into a plastic bottle of the sort that when squeezed ejects liquid through a small nozzle. If you can't find one of these bottles, paste a strip of black paper around the lighter-fuel container to disguise its appearance.

When the saturated center of a cotton handkerchief (don't use one made from synthetic fibers) is touched by a lighted match, a veritable blast of flame is produced. Beat it out quickly and crumple the cloth. If the flame flares for only a few seconds, it will not even scorch the handkerchief.

INDESTRUCTIBLE HANDKERCHIEF

In this variation of the preceding feat, the burning of the handkerchief leads to more complications. Beating out the flame, the embarrassed magician jams the handkerchief into his pocket. Then he reconsiders the situation. Perhaps the damage wasn't as great as he had imagined.

He takes out the handkerchief and opens it to see. A charred hole in the middle so distresses him that he thrusts it away again. But not for long. Recovering his confidence, he puts the handkerchief into a paper bag, announcing that he will restore the cloth to its original condition.

Briskly rubbing the bag between his open palms, he smiles. The smile fades when he pulls the handkerchief from the bag. While there is no trace of a burn, the once square cloth is now a long narrow strip. Surprised by this turn of events, he returns the cloth to the bag, gathers the top together, then fastens it with a rubber band.

Giving the bag to an onlooker, the magician stands several feet away, and claps his hands. "Open the bag and take out the handkerchief," he instructs. Seemingly a miracle has occurred —the burned and distorted material has mysteriously changed back into an unsullied handkerchief.

Required for this routine, in addition to a container of lighter fuel and a book of matches, are two matching handkerchiefs, one with a charred hole at its center; a strip of white cloth, two inches wide and five feet long; a paper bag; and several rubber bands.

Compress the burned handkerchief compactly. Tuck it up into the top corner of your right-hand trouser pocket. Roll the long strip of cloth into a snug ball. Put this inside the paper bag; then fold the bag so that you can carry it in the inside pocket of your jacket. Put the container of lighter fuel inside your left-hand trouser pocket, the book of matches and five rubber bands in your right-hand coat pocket, and the unprepared handkerchief in your right hip pocket.

After you have set fire to the saturated center of the unprepared handkerchief, beat out the flame, then jam the handkerchief deep into your right trouser pocket. Bring out the duplicate and display the charred hole. Then push it back into the top corner of your pocket and take out the crumpled but undamaged handkerchief.

Your left hand removes the paper bag from your inside coat pocket. Your right hand thrusts the handkerchief into the bag. After you have rubbed the sides of the bag between the palms of your hands, reach in for the end of the cloth strip. Pull this out to its full extent as it unrolls from the bag.

While holding the strip with your right hand, your thumb and fingers gather the cloth. This is seemingly returned to the bag, but, once your hand is inside, your fingers close around the cloth. When your hand goes to the right-hand pocket for a rubber band, the strip goes with it and is left in the pocket. I have discovered that when five rubber bands are in this pocket it is easier to find one quickly.

After the top of the bag has been closed with the rubber band, an onlooker holds the bag over his head. When the magician claps his hands, the spectator, not the magician, takes the restored handkerchief from the bag. The spectator can keep the empty bag as a souvenir.

Though no humorous remarks are made, this is a funny trick. Situation comedy pleases an audience, especially when, for a short time at least, the trick appears to have failed.

Note that the necessary props are carried by the magician in different pockets. No one can see or touch them until the show begins.

Sorcery with silk, photographed by Charles Reynolds, during the Indian Magic portion of Christopher's Wonders *in New York.*

THE RIVAL MAGICIAN

This burning routine is based on a different method. I designed it for television. Announcer Durward Kirby was my foil. He was not told what I would do. I wanted the sequence to surprise him as much as the audience. He was to wear a white handkerchief in the breast pocket of his coat and to attempt to repeat a trick after I had performed it.

The encounter began when I set fire to the center of his handkerchief, then restored it. Durward promptly said he could do this, too. He took my handkerchief, held it as I had held his, then lighted the cloth. Though he used the same gestures and almost the same words, the result was a hole in my handkerchief. After due annoyance on my part, I magically repaired the damage.

An extra handkerchief and a gimmick are involved in this presentation. (A gimmick is a secret device.) In this case the three-inch-long gimmick was made from a six-inch circular piece of white cloth. The illustration shows how it looks after the bottom has been gathered together and tied with a white thread.

GIMMICK

Fig. 1

THUMB
PRESSES
GIMMICK
AND
HANDKERCHIEF
TOGETHER SO THAT
THEY APPEAR AS ONE.

Fig. 2

LEFT HAND PULLS THE
BREAST POCKET OPEN.
THUMB BRINGS DUPLICATE
HANDKERCHIEF FORWARD
IN THE POCKET, SO THAT
IT WILL NOT BE PUSHED
DOWN WHEN THE BURNT
HANDKERCHIEF GOES IN.

Previous to the performance, I had folded the extra handkerchief in half, then in quarters, eighths, sixteenths, and finally, thirty-seconds, and put it out of sight in the breast pocket of my jacket. Behind the concealed handkerchief, I inserted the matching one, with a portion protruding. A cigarette lighter was readily accessible in my side pocket.

As I stood on the announcer's right during the show, the curled fingers of my right hand hid the gimmick. Reaching for his handkerchief with my left hand, I grasped the center between my right thumb and forefingers, secretly pressing the gimmick to the cloth, then transferred the handkerchief to my left hand.

My left fingers closed around the material, so that only the gimmick extended above my hand. I set the gimmick afire, allowing the cloth to burn just enough for the audience to realize what was happening. Then I beat out the flame with my right hand (still holding the lighter between thumb and index finger). During the course of this action, the three other fingers of my right hand closed around the gimmick and took it away, while my left hand bunched up the handkerchief. Keeping my eyes on the handkerchief, I dropped the lighter and the gimmick in my side pocket.

Passing the handkerchief to Kirby, I asked him to grip it firmly, then wiggled my fingers above his hand as I said the magic words, "A cautious conjurer has fire insurance." I opened the handkerchief between my hands to show that it had not been damaged.

Kirby slipped the handkerchief back into his pocket and winked. He said he could do the trick, too—with my handkerchief. I backed slightly away with my hand on my breast pocket, but he was too quick for me and pulled out the handkerchief.

He borrowed my lighter and applied the flame. Snuffing out the fire, he gave the handkerchief to me to hold. Despite his gestures and words, when I opened the handkerchief, there was a hole in its middle.

Feigning annoyance, I jammed the handkerchief into my breast pocket and started to walk away. Then, with a smile, I removed the handkerchief, squeezed it, and restored it.

This was possible because when I put the burned handkerchief into my pocket, I pushed it down and brought the upper portion of the duplicate handkerchief into view. This was the handkerchief I removed and "restored."

FAST AND LOOSE

No advance preparation is needed for this excellent trick: A double knot is tied with the diagonal ends of a handkerchief, and at the magician's command, the knot dissolves. Houdini often performed this feat to create the illusion that he could make the tightest knot disappear. On stage, he actually struggled and strained, exerting maximum muscular force, to release himself from challenge restraints, but a word was sufficient to make the handkerchief knot melt away—or so it seemed.

Fig. 1

RIGHT HAND PUTS "X" POINT OF END "B" OVER "Y" POINT OF END "A".

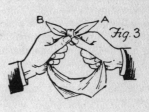

Fig. 3

RIGHT HAND MOVES UP AND BOTH HANDS HOLD "KNOT" FIRMLY.

Fig. 2

RIGHT HAND BRINGS HANDKERCHIEF UP TO AND OVER END "A".

SPECTATOR'S → KNOT

Fig. 4

SPECTATOR HAVING TIED HIS KNOT, THE PERFORMER'S RIGHT HAND BRINGS UP CORNER "C" AND DRAPES IT OVER THE KNOT.

Grasp the diagonal ends of the handkerchief, three inches from the corners, between the thumbs and fingers, as shown in the illustration. Bring the end in your right hand over and across the end in your left hand, lifting the left-hand thumb, then replacing it to hold the point where the two cross firmly. Immediately the right-hand fingers lift the handkerchief over the end extending from the left hand. This is what you would do to tie an overhand knot. As the right end of the handkerchief is, however, *over,* not under, the left end, the knot is not made. It only appears to be formed because the left thumb and fingers are holding the point of crossing securely.

As soon as you have tied this "knot," move your right thumb and index finger closer to it, pulling with right-hand fingers as the thumb and index finger grip the cloth.

Ask a spectator to tie a second knot. Suggest that he tie it as securely as possible. The harder he tugs on the ends, the stronger the finish of the feat will be.

Release your right hand and cover the knot with a free corner of the handkerchief. Invite the spectator to grasp the knot through the handkerchief. When he does so, release the grip of your left-hand thumb and fingers.

Exclaim, "Dissolve!" Take the remaining free corner of the handkerchief in your hand, pull it quickly from between the spectator's fingers, and toss the handkerchief into the air. Catch it as it falls, then show that the knot has disappeared.

SIX ENDS

Max Malini sometimes said, "Do you know this handkerchief has six corners? Please help me tie two of them together." He covered the knot, tied as described above, with a fold of the handkerchief, then with the aid of the same volunteer, he tied a second double knot. After he covered this, he found two more free corners. "Two here and four that are tied." He shook the handkerchief, then opened it out. "Not only have the knots dissolved but the extra corners have disappeared." The extra corners, of course, were those that had first been tied, then freed as he reached in the folds.

SLIPKNOTS

There is another way to dissolve double knots. It works best with silk or pure nylon handkerchiefs. After a spectator has tied two overhand knots, one above the other, the performer says he will make them tighter. Holding the tip of one end of the handkerchief in one hand and grasping a piece of the same end below the knot in the other, he tugs at the handkerchief. Rather than securing the knot, this action trips it, so that the other end is *around* the first one, not tied to it.

The resulting slipknot can be dissolved by pushing it firmly forward with the thumb below it as the fingers grip the cloth. This release is effected as the other hand drapes the handkerchief over the knot.

UNLINKING THE CHAIN

Once a performer has gained proficiency in the previous method, he can present a striking variation. A volunteer ties six handkerchiefs of as many colors end to end diagonally. After each double knot has been made, the magician, in "tightening" it, trips the knot. Then as he gathers the chain of silks, one by one, between his hands, he secretly releases the ends. The silks drop separately, at his command, onto a table or chair.

TIED AND UNTIED INSTANTLY

Magicians familiar with the methods described above were puzzled by a new technique I devised for instant releases and knottings. First a double knot, tied by a spectator, dissolved without cover; then the knot reappeared, and finally, while holding the handkerchief in one hand, I caused the knot instantly to untie again.

Magicians were deceived, because they didn't realize that I had not slipped the knot and retied it; that because I had used a gimmick, the original knot remained firm throughout the sequence.

The gimmick, in this case, is an extra end. A tight overhand knot is tied four inches in from the corner of another handkerchief; this portion is snipped away just below the knot.

Fold the gimmick in half and conceal it in the curled fingers of your right hand before you perform.

Display a pocket handkerchief, holding it a few inches from one corner between the left-hand thumb and index finger, with the other fingers partially closed around the material.

Bring your right hand over the left, encircling the handkerchief below your left hand with the first two right fingers. Slide

Despite the illustration on this 1868 playbill, Robert Heller did not have wings, and though billed as an American, he was an Englishman.

the fingers down until they are three inches from the diagonal tip. Bring the right hand up adjacent to the left hand. This action automatically folds the end of the handkerchief. The right-hand fingers close around it, pressing it firmly against the concealed knotted base of the gimmick.

The left-hand fingers reach into the right hand and bring what seems to be the end of the handkerchief into view. Actually this is the upper section of the gimmick.

With three inches of the handkerchief extending from each thumb and index finger, the magician invites a spectator to tie the ends with two knots, one above the other.

To create the illusion that the double knot dissolves, push the knot quickly into the right hand with the left thumb, then rapidly slide the closed fingers of the left hand along the handkerchief to the left. This pulls the concealed end from the right hand and whips it to the left where it is grasped by the left-hand fingers.

You will not appreciate this illusion until you have tried it.

The second phase of the feat is as fast as the first. The left hand darts its end of the handkerchief to the right hand. The right fingers hold the end firmly against the concealed knotted base of the gimmick. The thumb and index finger open as the left hand, which immediately circles the cloth, pulls the concealed knot tied by the spectator back into view.

For the final move, the left hand releases the handkerchief. It is held by the right fingers with the knot above the index finger. Two things now happen simultaneously.

As far as the audience is concerned, the magician simply shakes his hand with a snap, and the knot dissolves. As the hand is snapped, however, the right fingers release the end of the handkerchief they have been pressing to the knotted base of the gimmick and the right thumb moves forward to slide over the knot and conceal it.

IMAGINATION

"If you use your imagination," the magician says, "you can follow what I am about to do. If you have a really vivid imagination, you can almost see me doing it."

Pantomiming the removal of two objects from his pocket, he continues, "Here is a blue silk handkerchief and a red silk handkerchief. I tie them together and put them in this glass." He does these actions, then asks a spectator to hold the invisible glass.

"May I borrow your yellow handkerchief?" he asks as he approaches a woman. He pantomimes taking the handkerchief from her. "Watch closely." He rolls the invisible silk into an invisible ball, then tosses it toward the invisible glass held by the real spectator.

"The yellow handkerchief is not only in the glass," the magician states as he moves toward it and seems to reach for a corner of one of the invisible silks, "but—as you can see—it is tied between the red and the blue!"

As the words, "you can see" are spoken, three silks, red, yellow, and blue, knotted end to end, suddenly appear dangling from his fingertips.

To prepare for this feat, tie a yellow silk handkerchief by its diagonal corners between one that is red and another that is dark blue. Fasten one end of a fourteen-inch length of thin but strong black thread to the corner of the blue handkerchief diagonally across from the knot.

Fold the outer corners inward, then fold these folds inward on each of the three silks. Starting with the red silk, roll them up into a tight ball. Conceal it under your right armpit. Tie the free end of the thread extending from the blue handkerchief to the top button of your closed jacket. If the thread is too short, use a longer one.

When you pantomime reaching for the glass with your left hand, follow this action with your eyes. Meanwhile, your right thumb is secretly inserted under the thread that runs from the coat button to your armpit.

The moment you wish the string of silks to appear, lift your right elbow slightly from your side and move your right hand quickly forward. This will bring the ball of silks from its place of concealment to your fingertips. From there, the three handkerchiefs cascade into view.

EXPANSION

I devised this presentation for a sales meeting. A manufacturer, whose products had been available only in the eastern part of the United States, wanted me to stress that his wares were now to be distributed nationwide.

I took a small silk from my pocket. On it was the firm's insignia. "A year ago, only a limited number of Americans recognized this design," I said. "In a few months, due to an advertising campaign that includes network television, national magazines, and newspapers from coast to coast, it will be known everywhere." I rolled the little silk between my hands as I talked; on the word "everywhere," it instantly expanded to giant proportions.

Simplicity was the keynote of the demonstration. Two thin silk handkerchiefs were used—one, twelve inches square, the other, thirty-six inches square. A corner of the first was firmly sewn to a corner of the second. Holding the corner of the larger silk that was attached to the smaller one in my right hand, and the diagonal corner of the same square in my left one, I twirled the silk held between my hands to form a more compact, rope-like length. Then I folded this with small pleats and wound the last ten inches around the packet to hold it in place. Prepared this way, I concealed the bundle with closed right fingers and held the corner of the smaller silk, which had been sewn to the larger one, between my thumb and index finger.

Upon being introduced at the sales conference, I displayed the small insignia between my hands, and as I talked, I brought my hands together and forced the small silk into my left hand. I closed those fingers around it and gripped the point where the two silks were fastened together between my left thumb and index finger. When I mentioned expansion, I whipped the concealed silk from my right hand and, as it expanded, held it up by the two top corners so that it could be seen throughout the hotel ballroom.

PERFECT COLOR REPRODUCTION

Appearing at a luncheon given in honor of Ben Dalgin, then director of art and reproduction for *The New York Times,* I spoke of the marvels of color processing. Ben, I said, was a member of the Society of American Magicians; his knowledge of magic, as I would demonstrate, had been applied in his work for *The Times.* I displayed six small silk handkerchiefs of different colors, rolled them up, then secured them with two rubber bands. When I pulled away the elastics, the six small silks blended into one large one. On it was an exact replica of a color photograph.

I have used the same routine to produce a large silk banner with a slogan on it in six colors, and to convert six hues into a futuristic design.

The large varicolored silk is rolled into a small ball, and encircled by a rubber band. This is carried in the right-hand trouser pocket, along with six rubber bands. At the start of the trick the smaller silks may be taken from the performer's left-hand pocket, or introduced in a more interesting way—popping into view, one by one, from the breast pocket of his coat.

To prepare for the latter effect, tuck one corner of the first silk square into your breast pocket, twist the extending diagonal corner twice around a corner of the second handkerchief. Push these silks deep down into your pocket, twist the corner of the third silk twice around the extending corner of the second one. Continue this process until all are concealed from view.

During the show, pull out the top silk, and the next one will pop up. As the silks have been twisted together, not tied, the removal of one brings the corner of the next from the pocket. After all have been taken out, bunch them tightly together in your left hand, hold the bundle up for display as your right hand goes to your pocket for a rubber band. While there, your right hand closes around the large silk, which is brought out, concealed by your closed fingers, while your hand openly displays the rubber band held between the tips of the thumb and index finger.

The reason I suggested you should carry six rubber bands in this pocket is so that you can find one without fumbling. Snap the rubber band around the bundle of small silks, then take the bundle in your right hand to display it. As you pick up the bundle, press the concealed large silk against it. The colors of the small silks are the same as those in the large varicolored silk. When the two bundles are held together tightly, they will therefore appear to be one. Transfer the large silk to your left hand, taking only the large one and closing the fingers of your right hand around the bundle of small silks. Now raise your left hand above your head and follow it with your eyes as you reach with your right hand for another rubber band, leaving the bundle of small silks in your pocket as you take out the elastic.

After you have snapped the second rubber band around the

large silk, toss the silk high in the air and catch it. Pull off the rubber bands and allow the compressed silk to bulk up before you grasp it by two corners, holding your hands apart as the silk opens out so that the audience can see its size and the design on its surface.

A crumpled piece of paper changes into a dollar bill during Milbourne Christopher's hour of TV magic with Mike Wallace and Joyce Davidson.

Money Magic

Tricks with money have a special appeal. Everyone would like to pluck coins from nowhere or convert dollar bills into tens. Some feats in this category are difficult to do; others can be mastered with little effort. Often the simplest sleights are the most effective. One you can learn quickly frequently evokes more astonishment than one that requires months of practice. All that really matters is the effect on the audience.

The first four tricks in this chapter are based on a single sleight. It is the same sleight already described in "Undercover Operation," the trick with two squares of cardboard torn from a matchbook cover.

SUDDENLY—SILVER

Holding one edge of a dollar bill between the thumb and index finger of his right hand, the magician displays both sides of the bill, then folds it into thirds. When he tilts the bill slightly, a half-dollar rolls out from its center. This quick and surprising close-up feat stands on its own as an impromptu puzzler, but it is also a strong opening for a routine of intimate conjuring.

To prepare, fold a dollar bill around a fifty-cent piece. Place the wrapped coin in your right-hand trouser pocket. When you are ready to perform, take out the bill, tilting it so that the coin will drop into your curled fingers and be hidden from view. Using both hands, smooth out the dollar bill, then hold it near the edge of one of its long sides between your right-hand thumb and fingers.

The half-dollar is under the bill, pressed against it by the tip of your middle finger. The thumb is on the top side of the bill. Turn your hand to the right to display the reverse side of the bill. As you do so, slide the coin inward with the tip of your middle finger. Most of the fifty-cent piece will be concealed by your slightly curled and adjacent first three fingers. The small portion of the coin that remains on the bill is covered by the tips of the three fingers.

Turn your hand to the right, sliding the coin back into its original position, and spreading your fingers when the bill is face-up. In this way you show both sides of the bill and of your hand without the coin being seen.

While you do so, say, "At one time the words 'silver certificate' were printed on every American dollar, and you could get the silver on demand." Fold back the top and bottom thirds of the paper money, bringing the coin inside the fold, and continue, "Today only a magician can produce hard cash." Strike the bill on the table. An unexpected thud is heard. Tilt the bill as you say, "Though not as much as before," and allow the half-dollar to roll out and fall onto the table.

PAYING THE BILL

The technique employed to conceal a coin works equally well with paper money that has been folded and creased into a small, tight package. Have a folded twenty-dollar bill concealed by the closed last three fingers of your right hand when you reach for another sort of bill—the one for your luncheon. Pick up the bill with your fingers (and the paper money) under it and your thumb on top. Casually display both sides of the restaurant bill, then fold it in half so the paper money will be inside the fold. Tilt the folded bill and the package of money will drop from the center. Give the money and the bill to the waiter.

RAPID BANKING

"I had intended to pay for a purchase with this," the magician says as he displays both sides of a bank check. "The clerk insisted on cash." The magician crumples up the check and is about to throw it aside when he recalls what happened next. "Strangely enough, when I opened the crumpled paper, I found a twenty dollar bill inside it."

As you can see there are many uses for the skill that enables you to show both sides of an object, then make an unexpected production from it. While writing this book, I devised another trick, one that fascinates owners of credit cards.

INSTANT CASH

To prepare for this feat, fold a crisp new twenty dollar bill into sixteenths. Insert it under a plastic credit card in your wallet.

To present it, take out your wallet and withdraw the credit card, holding it with your fingers—and the concealed paper money—at the back and your thumb on the name side.

"This is a most unusual credit card though it looks like thousands of others." Show it back and front, then continue, "If I need cash quickly, I simply press on the surface and the money is dispatched to me instantly." As you speak, the folded dollar bill materializes between the tips of the thumb and index finger of your left hand.

After showing both sides of the card with your right hand, bring your hands together. The right thumb and middle finger hold the card. The thumb is on the upper surface; the tip of the middle finger presses the concealed money to the lower side.

The fingers of the left hand go under the card as the left thumb is about to press down on the surface. Before the thumb moves, the right middle finger slides the bill across under the card so the left fingers can take it.

Now, while holding the card securely between the right thumb and index finger, touch the surface of the card with the ball of your left thumb, and bend the card upward with your left fingers. The bill appears suddenly between the tips of the thumb and the fingers, as the card, still gripped by the right thumb and middle finger, snaps past the left fingers.

The sudden appearance of the bill creates the illusion that it materialized instantly.

THE ALCHEMIST'S SECRET

Arthur Cowan had retired from the vaudeville stage long before I met him. Short, bald, and reminiscent of Max Malini in manner, he was a magnificent showman.

I remember the first time I saw Cowan perform at a party. He asked his host for a box of matches, emptied it of its contents, dropped a dime into the open tray, then snapped the box shut.

He shook the box several times. We could hear the dime rattling against the sides. Then he put the box down on a coffee table, and walked away several feet from it.

"Alchemists claimed they could convert baser metal into gold," Cowan began. "I have read about this, but I have never seen it done. Perhaps I'll never be able to rival their skill, but I can dematerialize silver—and at a distance."

He turned toward the matchbox and closed his eyes. When he opened them, he told me to pick up the box and shake it. I did. There was no sound. "Push out the tray. Look inside," he continued. I did. The box was empty.

Cowan's presentation is an example of how a simple trick can be made into a near miracle. To prepare for the feat, get an oblong matchbox, the sort used for wooden matches. Open the drawer, then press upward with your thumb against the inner side of the cover. This causes the cover to arch slightly. With your thumb on the top of the cover, press down until the cover is almost, but not quite, straight.

This, Cowan had done earlier that evening as he took the box from the coffee table to light his cigar. An hour later, when he asked for a matchbox, this was the one the host gave him.

After he dropped the dime into the empty tray and closed the box, Cowan held the box between the fingers of his right hand as he shook the coin from side to side. Just before he put the box on the table, he held it upright, squeezed the sides, and out slipped the dime into his waiting fingers. In the act of placing the box, label side up, on the table, he moved his index finger to the top and pressed down, straightening the slight arch.

Did Cowan produce the dime as soon as the spectators were

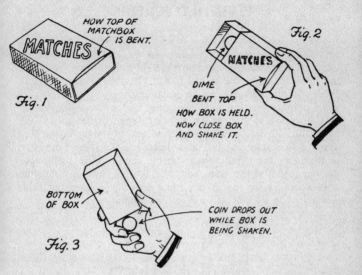

HOW TOP OF
MATCHBOX
IS BENT.

MATCHES

Fig. 1

Fig. 2

MATCHES

DIME
BENT TOP
HOW BOX IS HELD.
NOW CLOSE BOX
AND SHAKE IT.

BOTTOM
OF BOX

COIN DROPS OUT
WHILE BOX IS
BEING SHAKEN.

Fig. 3

convinced it had disappeared? No, he did not. Instead he asked for a pack of cards. Removing the cards from their case he dealt two facedown on the coffee table. "Turn one face-up," he told a young woman. She did. "Put your hand on the other one while I concentrate," he continued. He shut his eyes and relaxed for about fifteen seconds. "Turn over the other card," he said, after he had opened his eyes. She did. The dime that had disappeared was under it.

"What would you have done if she had turned the card covering the dime face-up?" I asked Cowan months afterward. "Accepted the applause then, instead of later," he replied with a smile.

The dime had been concealed by the curled middle and ring fingers of Cowan's hand since it had dropped from the box. When he dealt two cards face-down, the coin was loaded beneath the first one as his right fingers placed the card on the table.

I said I had not heard the slightest sound as the dime reached the table. "That," he explained, "is the most difficult part of the trick, but you can master the knack with practice." If the table is covered with a cloth before the trick begins, however, less skill is needed.

FIVEFOLD SURPRISE

The magician folds a piece of white paper into a small package. As he squeezes it in his left hand, he reaches with his right hand into his pocket for a cigarette lighter. Igniting it, he passes the flame beneath the closed hand. The heat works wonders. The paper changes into a five dollar bill.

To prepare for this trick, you must fold a five dollar bill so that it appears to be a blank piece of paper. To learn the fold, place the bill on a table, green side up, as shown in the first illustration. Crease the bill, as indicated in the second drawing, so that only the white appears at the center. Then fold under the remainder at the sides, top, and bottom, leaving the white area alone visible, as in the third drawing. Crease the folds sharply; then the bill will not unfold prematurely.

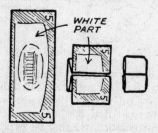

WHITE PART

Before you perform, conceal the bill in your right hand, hiding it behind your curled fingers. Have a blank piece of white paper about half the size of a dollar bill in your right-hand coat pocket, along with a cigarette lighter. Take the paper from your coat pocket and pass it to your left hand. Show the paper on both sides, then bring your hands together to fold it. Crease it into a packet the size of the concealed bill. Hold this between your right thumb and index finger.

Draw attention to your left hand by extending it and opening your fingers. Show the audience both the back and the front. While your eyes follow this action, your right hand drops naturally to your side, and you switch the paper for the folded five dollar bill.

Turn your eyes to the right as you raise your right hand with the blank area of the bill extending from your thumb and fingers. Put the "paper" into your left hand, closing your hand immediately.

Reach for the cigarette lighter, leaving the paper in the pocket as you bring out the lighter. Ignite the lighter, hold it fleetingly under your closed left hand, then drop the lighter back in your pocket. Open your closed left fingers, then unfolding the five dollar bill with both hands, smooth it out and display its two sides.

MULTIPLYING BILLS

This classic production is a logical follow-up to exhibiting the five dollar bill. Say that the Treasury Department has learned about your new printing process and is seriously considering using it to replace government presses.

"They're even more intrigued by another of my inventions," the magician continues. He pulls up both sleeves, then rubbing the bill briskly, produces six more from it.

To prepare for this finale, compress six five dollar bills into a small, tight ball. Conceal the ball in a fold of your coat just above the bend of your left elbow. When your arm is bent even slightly, the wad of bills will be held in place and out of view.

After changing the paper into a dollar bill, hold the bill in your left hand. Your right hand pulls up your left sleeve by grasping the cloth and tugging at the sleeve. Your right hand also takes the packet of money from the fold. Once the sleeve has been pulled up, the right hand takes the five dollar bill from the left hand, and the left hand pulls up the right sleeve. The hands then come together to rub the bill, and to open up the packet the fingers of your right hand have concealed, so that the illusion is created that one five dollar bill has changed into seven.

COIN CONVERSION

Banks will give you a dollar bill for a silver dollar. Coin dealers will add a premium for the silver. Unless the silver dollar is a rare one, however, you will never be offered ten times its original value.

Magicians are not limited by current exchange rates. Whenever you wish, you can convert a silver dollar into a ten dollar bill.

That is, you can if beforehand you conceal a tightly folded bill behind the coin. Then display the coin held in your finger-tips as depicted in the illustration. The folded bill is pressed against the coin by your left thumb. Change the coin and the hidden bill to your right hand. Once more the bill is hidden by the silver dollar.

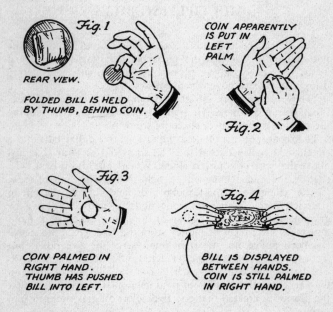

Fig. 1

REAR VIEW.

FOLDED BILL IS HELD BY THUMB, BEHIND COIN.

COIN APPARENTLY IS PUT IN LEFT PALM

Fig. 2

Fig. 3

COIN PALMED IN RIGHT HAND. THUMB HAS PUSHED BILL INTO LEFT.

Fig. 4

BILL IS DISPLAYED BETWEEN HANDS. COIN IS STILL PALMED IN RIGHT HAND.

Bring the coin back to your left hand, turning your right hand on the way so that its closed fingers are above the silver dollar and the thumb is beneath it, and only the end of the coin can be seen from the front. Your left fingers close as the right thumb pulls the coin back and the right fingers push the folded bill into the left palm.

Raise your left hand a few inches and squeeze your fingers together. Open your fingers to reveal the paper money. Display it a few seconds, then unfold the bill between your hands.

You can, if you wish, palm the silver dollar; that is, grip it in your palm. The coin can be concealed just as easily, however, by curling your right-hand fingers around it.

Release the ten dollar bill and let it fall to the table. Reach for your billfold in your right hip pocket. Leave the coin there as you withdraw the wallet. Then casually pick up the money and put it in your billfold.

If you are in a generous mood, you can offer to sell the ten dollar bill for half its value. Most onlookers will be leery, having heard that counterfeit banknotes are widely circulated. Should someone buy it, he will certainly tell his friends about the magician who converted a silver dollar into a ten dollar bill, then sold it for five. Oh, yes, ask for a receipt after the sale. Then you can take a five-dollar deduction on your next income tax report for advertising expenses.

SILVER TO COPPER

The magician displays a dime in one hand and a penny in the other. He directs attention to the dime by raising his left hand slightly and saying, "Silver." Then he turns his attention to the penny and, raising his right hand slightly, says, "Copper." At the word "Pass," the two coins change places almost instantaneously.

To prepare for this trick, solder a dime to a penny and a penny to a dime, as shown in the illustration. The drawing also indicates how the coins are displayed so that only one coin of each set is visible.

It would take considerable practice to exchange a dime displayed by one hand for a penny concealed by the fingers. The soldered coins are easier to handle. Stand in front of a mirror with a coin displayed in each hand, and the backs of your hands turned to the mirror. The visible coins are held between the thumbs and first two fingers of each hand. Turn the hands simultaneously at the wrists, the right hand to the left, and the left hand to the right. As the right hand turns, the tips of the index finger and the thumb continue to hold the attached coins, but the tip of the middle finger moves down and pushes the concealed penny to the right, then reaches up to pull the visible dime down. This causes the penny to appear and the dime to be concealed where the penny was a moment before. Immediately the right hand turns to the right to display the dime. The left hand, meanwhile, has switched the visible dime for the concealed penny in the other set of soldered coins.

Practice until you can make the changes rapidly. As the thumbs hide the concealed coins, you can turn your hands to show your palms after the trick is over.

TRANSPOSITION

The magician drops a penny into the open drawer of an empty matchbox. Closing the drawer, he gives the box to a spectator. Standing some distance away, the performer then puts his right hand into his trouser pocket and brings into view a dime which he displays at his fingertips. The dime changes into a penny; the penny in the matchbox changes into a dime.

A dime was concealed behind the penny. When the penny apparently fell into the drawer of the matchbox, the thumb pulled the penny back, and the concealed dime fell instead. The matchbox is held high enough so that spectators cannot see inside the drawer. Hearing the coin fall, they assume it is the penny they have seen earlier.

Reaching into his right-hand trouser pocket for a set of coins soldered edge to edge, as described in the previous trick, the magician leaves the penny there and brings out the joined coins with the dime in view at his fingertips.

A swing of his hand reverses the coins. The penny appears where the dime had been a moment before.

When the spectator opens the matchbox he had been holding, he finds that the penny has disappeared and a dime has taken its place.

INVISIBLE EXTRACTION

This is a variation of Transposition with a totally unexpected conclusion. After a twenty-five cent piece has been put in the drawer of a matchbox, the magician snaps several rubber bands around the box, then places it on a table.

"I think you will agree," he says, "that it would be impossible for me to extract the quarter without touching the box."

Standing several feet away, he continues, "The quarter will pass invisibly into my trouser pocket." He pauses, then gestures first toward the box, then toward his pocket. Reaching into the pocket, he brings something out in his closed hand. "Another miracle," he proclaims, opening his fingers to reveal a heap of pennies.

He counts them rapidly into his free hand, frowning when he discovers there are twenty-four, not twenty-five. "I must have done that too quickly," he explains with a smile. He asks an onlooker to remove the elastics from the box, then open the drawer. The twenty-fifth penny is where the quarter had been.

To prepare for this presentation, carry twenty-four pennies in your otherwise empty right-hand trouser pocket, the matchbox in your left-hand jacket pocket, and the quarter, a penny, and six rubber bands in your right-hand jacket pocket.

When performing, show that the matchbox is empty. Hold it with the drawer extending in your left hand. Bring out the quarter with the penny hidden behind it. Hold the two coins between the tips of your right thumb and first two fingers. The thumb rests on the quarter. Show both sides of the quarter by turning your hand to the left and sliding the penny inward with your middle finger. As you turn the hand to the right again, the middle finger slides the coin back under the quarter. (This is the same sleight that has been described at the beginning of this chapter.)

When you apparently drop the quarter into the drawer of the matchbox, the back of your right hand is toward the spectators. Slide the quarter inward with your thumb, and let the penny fall. The spectators do not see the coin dropping into the drawer, but they hear its fall.

Close the drawer, then reach with your right hand for the rubber bands, leaving the quarter in your jacket pocket as you remove the elastics.

Snap the first rubber band around the box to keep the drawer

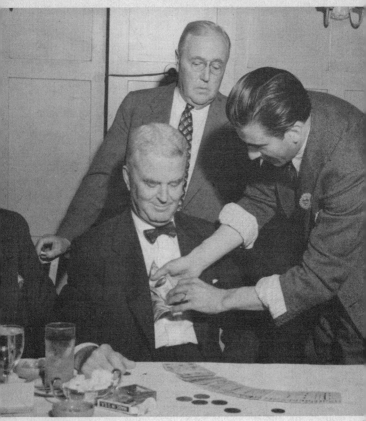

Paul Rosini changed First National Bank president Lyman E. Wakefield's dollar bills into twenties at the Minneapolis Club in Minnesota.

closed. Wind the others around the sides as well as the ends. Shake the box before you place it on the table. The rattling noise conveys the impression that the quarter is still there.

When you say you have caused the coin to pass invisibly into your trouser pocket, reach for the twenty-four pennies. Close your fingers around them before withdrawing your hand. I suggested earlier that you keep this pocket otherwise empty. You can scoop up the coins quicker if there are no obstacles in your way.

After displaying the pennies and counting them, do not approach the matchbox. If you took off the rubber bands, this would weaken the climax. When the spectator finds the missing penny in the drawer, ask him to take it out and hold it up so that everyone can see it.

EXPENSIVE SMOKE

Tearing away a corner of a spectator's dollar bill, the magician gives the corner to the owner of the bill, then crumples up the bill and sets it afire. He lights a cigarette from the flame as the money is reduced to ashes. A moment later, he breaks open the cigarette he has been smoking. In it is the dollar with a missing corner. The bill is returned to the owner. The corner he has been holding fits the bill perfectly.

This feat requires a filter-tip cigarette, a pair of small tweezers, an almost new dollar bill, a bill-size piece of paper torn from the newspaper reproduction of a photograph, two matchbooks, and an ashtray.

With the tweezers remove the filter material and some of the tobacco above it from the end of the cigarette. Crumple the dollar bill, then open it, and, while holding it lengthwise with the portrait side up, tear away the upper right corner. This jagged tear should begin an inch in from the end of the bill. Put the corner into the bottom fold of a closed matchbook, behind the striking surface, so that most of the corner extends up on the flap side. Place this matchbook in your right-hand jacket pocket, and the second matchbook in your left-hand one.

Crumple carefully the section from a newspaper reproduction of a photograph. If you have selected one with contrasting black and white portions, it can be crumpled to look like a dollar bill that has been wadded up with the green side turned inward. Put the crumpled paper ball in your right-hand jacket pocket, along with the matchbook that carries the corner of the dollar bill. Fold the dollar into eighths, then roll it up tightly, and insert it into the cigarette, pushing it until the upper end of the bill meets the tobacco and the lower end does not protrude from the tipped section of the cigarette. Place the prepared cigarette in your left-hand jacket pocket along with the unprepared matchbook.

Shortly before presenting this trick, stand with your hands in your coat pockets. Close the last two fingers of your right hand around the ball of newspaper. Then slide the corner of the dollar bill from the matchbook with your thumb and hold the corner above the crumpled newspaper with the tip of your curled middle finger. Take your hands from your pockets before you say you would like to borrow a dollar bill.

When an onlooker holds up a dollar, take it with your left hand, then transfer it to your right hand. It is to be kept there only momentarily, just long enough to position it, green side down, over the concealed corner. The left hand takes it again, fingers above and thumb below, with the thumb pressing the corner to the bill. As the left hand displays the bill, the right hand tears away the upper right corner. This piece should be approximately the same size and shape as the corner concealed behind the bill. The hands separate as the piece is ripped away. When they come together, it appears that the left hand takes the corner and the right hand takes the bill. Actually a switch of corners is made behind the bill. The right thumb retains the corner that was torn away behind the bill, and the corner that fits the bill in the cigarette is displayed at the tips of the left thumb and the first two fingers of the left hand.

Give the visible corner to the spectator. Then bunch up the dollar between your two hands with the hidden corner crumpled inside the bill. Reach with your empty left hand for the unprepared matchbook in your left-hand jacket pocket. When you bring it out, display it. With attention fixed on the matchbook, drop your right hand to your side. Switch the ball of newspaper that has been hidden by the curled fingers for the bill and retain the bill. Put the "dollar" into an ashtray with your right hand, then tear one of the matches from the folder. Light the "dollar," drop the match into the tray, put the matchbook—and the hidden dollar—into your right-hand side pocket.

While the "dollar" is burning, casually light the prepared cigarette from the flame. Take a few puffs, then cough. Look at

Milbourne Christopher presented the Triple Escape for the first time at a Society of American Magicians show at Hunter College in New York City.

the ashes in the tray, then at the cigarette. Snuff out the burning end in the ashtray, then hold up the cigarette and peel away the paper wrapping. Lift your eyebrows when you see the rolled dollar bill. Smooth out the bill between your hands and point to the part where a corner is missing. Give the bill to the owner of the original dollar. Ask him to fit the corner he has been holding to the bill and verify that the jagged edges coincide.

A few suggestions. At the start of the trick ask several spectators to hold dollar bills in the air. Take the one that most closely resembles the one you have loaded in the cigarette. Reach for it before the owner has time to note the serial number. It is difficult to tell one wadded bill from another. That is why I suggested that you crumple your dollar. This trick is better suited for a large audience than a small one. With many onlookers, usually at least three or four will offer dollar bills.

THE SHRINKING DOLLAR

Borrow a dollar, then crumple it into a ball, and roll the ball firmly between your hands. Say, "Once a dollar bill was worth a dollar." Open the bill but do not smoothe out the creases. "Years ago, however, its purchasing power diminished to ninety cents." Due to the kneading and compression, the bill will appear to have shrunk.

Ball it up again, roll it between your hands again, and once more open it carefully. It will appear to have become even smaller when you open it. "Today a dollar is worth even less. I could show you how it will look in the future, but you had better take it back before it disappears."

POKER-CHIP CONJURING

Strictly speaking, poker chips are not money, though they are used to represent money in card games. They can be carried as conveniently as coins and are handled in the same way. As a boy I produced poker chips instead of half-dollars at my fingertips and dropped them into an empty wastebasket rather than a metal pail as did T. Nelson Downs, Al Flosso, and other expert performers of the Miser's Dream.

Later I devised several close-up tricks with poker chips. Three are based on a single basic sleight. To learn it, hold three stacked chips in your right hand between your thumb, index, and middle fingertips, as shown in the illustration.

Bring the right hand to the left, turning it at the wrist, so that the chip that was uppermost is now at the bottom of the stack. Slide the top chip off into your left hand with your left thumb and index finger.

Immediately turn your right hand to the right, so attention is attracted to the bottom chip. Again bring the right hand to the left, turning it at the wrist, and slide off the top chip. Once more turn your right hand to the right, showing the underside of the remaining chip, then bring your hand to the left, and slide off this chip.

It will seem as if you have shown both sides of each chip. Actually you have displayed the *top* sides of all three chips, but only the *bottom* side of one.

COLOR-CHANGING CHIPS

Paste disks of colored paper on each of three white poker chips: red on one, yellow on the second, blue on the third. Stack the chips so that the colored spots are on the under sides, with the red at the bottom.

Using the basic sleight, appear to show that each white chip has a red spot on the under side. As the order of the chips is reversed during this procedure, you can say, "Change," and by repeating the sleight, show that the red stickers are now blue. Finally, tap the stack and say, "Various colors." Lift off the chips, one by one, turning them bottom side up to display blue, yellow, and red stickers.

SPIRIT MESSAGE

Two of the three chips in this variation are unprepared; a message is written beforehand on one side of the third chip. Turning the chip so that the side with the message is underneath, place it in the middle of the stack of three chips. Using the basic sleight, appear to show both sides of each chip. Place the stack bottom side up on the table. When the top chip is lifted, the message will appear on the surface of the chip beneath it.

CHIP PASSE PASSE

Six chips play a part in this presentation. Three have blue stickers on one side; three carry red stickers. Stack the chips in two heaps as follows: The bottom chip of the stack to the left has a blue sticker on its lower side; the two above it both have red. The stack to the right has a red, blue, blue sequence.

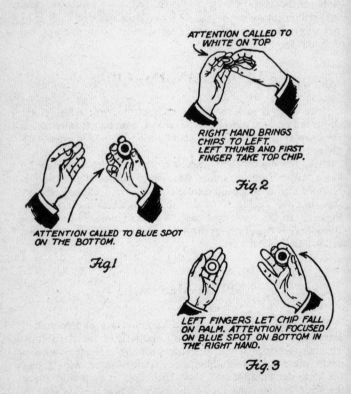

ATTENTION CALLED TO WHITE ON TOP

RIGHT HAND BRINGS CHIPS TO LEFT. LEFT THUMB AND FIRST FINGER TAKE TOP CHIP.

Fig. 2

ATTENTION CALLED TO BLUE SPOT ON THE BOTTOM.

Fig. 1

LEFT FINGERS LET CHIP FALL ON PALM. ATTENTION FOCUSED ON BLUE SPOT ON BOTTOM IN THE RIGHT HAND.

Fig. 3

Using the basic sleight, create the illusion that the stickers on the chips to the left are blue and those to the right are red. Sliding off the chips automatically brings the bottom chips to the top of each stack. The new order is blue, red, red . . . red, blue, blue.

Turn over the top chip of the stack at the left to display the blue sticker, reverse the upper chip of the right stack to show the red sticker. Take the chip with the blue sticker and put it on the table to the right. The one with the red sticker goes to the left. Turn up the remaining two chips in each stack. The stickers have changed color to match those that were moved.

Though I first performed this and the two preceding feats with poker chips, I later used half-dollars and substituted postage stamps for the colored disks. Magic with money is more fascinating.

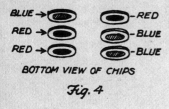

BLUE →   -RED
RED →   -BLUE
RED →   -BLUE

BOTTOM VIEW OF CHIPS

Fig. 4

ALL RED   ALL BLUE

Fig. 6

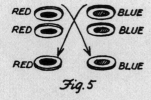

RED   BLUE
RED   BLUE

RED   BLUE

Fig. 5

Neil Brookes, manager of the Empire Theatre, Liverpool, and Mrs. E. M. Braddock, member of Parliament, participated in a Sealed Letter Test during the Christopher's Wonders *tour of Britain in 1961.*

Mental Magic

A mentalist is a magician who creates the illusion that he can send and receive thoughts, predict future events, or otherwise cause the mind to exert an influence in some seemingly inexplicable way. Though charlatans claim psychic powers, mentalists present their baffling feats for entertainment.

This phase of magic is increasingly popular. More people than ever before are interested in precognition, telepathy, and clairvoyance. Almost everyone seems to have had some kind of extrasensory experience that cannot be explained to his or her satisfaction. Some have seemed to sense accidents or other tragedies before they happened. Others think of a distant friend for the first time in years, and almost immediately receive a letter or a phone call from the person.

Dunninger, the most famous mentalist of modern times, once told me that he could reveal the shabby frauds of spirit mediums without losing his appeal to the masses, but if he were to admit that his own amazing feats were simply tricks, he would no longer be able to intrigue his audiences. Until the day he died, he maintained—to the public—that he had extraordinary thought-reading ability.

I hope my readers will follow Houdini's example, not Dunningers's. Houdini prefaced his performances with an honest disclaimer of possessing any supernormal powers—and he will be remembered long after other mystifiers have been forgotten.

Legitimate mentalists should at least allow audiences to make up their own minds as to the validity of the marvels they present.

CRYSTAL CHOICE

The mentalist announces that he will make a prediction. He picks up a large slate and a piece of chalk. Holding the slate so that the audience cannot see the movements of his right hand, he writes a word on it. Leaning the slate against the back of a chair, with the blank surface facing outward, he turns his attention to a volunteer from the audience. "Here," he says, displaying several newspapers, "are three different issues of *The Times.* Please take one. Open it to a page of classified advertisements, then fold the page so that I can hold the paper in one hand."

As the spectator follows these instructions, the mentalist displays a crystal ball. "Crystal balls have been used by seers for thousands of years," he continues. "They say they can see the future as they gaze into the crystal. If you have a vivid imagination, you can visualize distant scenes, strange events, and unfamiliar faces. I employ a crystal for another purpose . . . as a magnifying glass!"

Grasping in his left hand the folded newspaper provided by the volunteer, the mentalist holds the ball over the paper and invites the volunteer to read a word through the crystal. Sliding the ball to another part of the page, he asks the volunteer to read another one there.

"As I move the ball from the left of the page to the right, will someone call out, 'Stop!'" the performer asks. When the signal is given, the spectator by the mentalist's side is asked to read aloud the word the crystal magnifies.

"Earlier," the mentalist says, "I wrote down a prediction on the slate. I have not been near it since. Would you go to the slate and turn the writing on it to the front?" The word printed in large letters on the slate is the same as the one selected at random from the newspaper.

You need not meditate seven hours a day for seven years to

prepare for this feat. Nor is it necessary for you to fast, as some mystics do. Simply cut out a word from another copy of the newspaper you are going to use and fasten the word face-up to the center of a small piece of transparent tape. Press the tape firmly against the crystal and you will see the magnified word if you look through the opposite side of the crystal.

When the crystal ball is displayed, hold it with the prepared side down, your thumb over the tape and your fingers at the top of the ball.

The ball may now be freely displayed. Anyone peering into the ball will not be aware that it has been prepared.

As you move the ball across the newspaper page, turn the ball so that the taped word rests on the paper. When the volunteer looks through the ball, he will see this word enlarged.

The word fastened to the ball is the same as the one you printed on the slate at the start of the presentation. At first I pasted the word to the ball. Later I found that transparent tape made it easier to remove one word and substitute another for a subsequent performance.

WATER DIVINATION

What began as an after-dinner parlor trick developed into a stage mystery. Instead of a crystal ball, I used a glass of water. A spectator gazing directly down into the water could reveal the name of a playing card I had earlier written down on the under side of a menu.

The stage presentation has all the elements of exciting theatre. I ask for a volunteer, preferably a woman who has played a part in a school or community play.

When the spectator is by my side, I explain that she is to have the role of a gifted medium. If she follows my instructions, she will astonish the audience with her extrasensory ability.

I pour some water from a pitcher into a glass, then ask her what she sees in the glass. "Water." I put the bottom of the glass in the palm of her left hand, place the palm of her right hand over the top of the glass, then position the glass waist-high, a few inches away from her body.

Walking down into the audience with a large pad and a broad-tipped felt pen, I announce I will try to transmit thoughts to the medium. "Ancient diviners stared into a bowl of ink or water when a crystal ball was not available. The glass of water, held in the palm of the volunteer's hand, will serve as a focal point for her concentration."

Holding the pad so that the audience—but not the volunteer —can see what I write, I print a name—for example, Charles.

"Take your right hand away from the top of the glass," I instruct the volunteer; "gaze down into the water. I will send you three mental images. The first one is a name. Please concentrate; then spell it out."

The seeress gazes at the water and spells out C-H-A-R-L-E-S. I compliment her on her talent, then say I will write a three-digit number. The audience sees me tear off the first sheet of the pad, toss it aside, then write 482 on the second sheet.

The water-gazer has no difficulty in getting the numbers, 4-8-2.

I announce that I will write down the name of a city where I once performed. She correctly spells out B-E-L-É-M.

I return to the stage, praise her telepathic abilities, and ask the audience to give her an extra round of applause. As she returns to her seat, I add, "Please don't tell anyone how it was done, or everyone will tune in on our thoughts." This invariably produces laughter.

Use a glass with a thick bottom. Write the words and the numbers on the sticky side of an inch-square piece of Manila tape or a postage stamp. Wet the adhesive and fasten it on the bottom of the glass in the center. When water is poured into the glass, neither the adhesive nor the writing on it can be seen by anyone looking at the glass—unless they peer down from above into the water.

As soon as the volunteer removes her right hand from the top of the glass, she can see the three cues. She reveals the name, number, and city as she follows your instructions.

What seems to be a parting joke is the suggestion that she keep your secret. The chances are she will.

CONCENTRATE ON A CARD

Twenty or so members of the audience are asked to write down the name of a playing card on a slip of paper and then fold the paper in quarters concealing what they have written. The papers are then collected by a volunteer and brought to the platform. The volunteer mixes the folded papers, selects one, then concentrates on it as the mentalist looks through a pack of cards, and selects one. It is the card named on the paper.

There is an indentation on the upper side of a cardboard case of playing cards. It is there to aid in opening the flap. This cut-out half circle is employed for a different purpose in the feat described above. Write the name of a playing card on a two-inch square of paper. Fold the paper in half, then in quarters. Insert the paper into the closed case so that it rests between the flap and the front of the box, without extending over the top. When the performer's thumb is placed over the portion exposed at the indentation, it will hide the visible part of the paper. The thumb can also slide out the paper when needed.

Twenty or so pieces of paper, the same size as the one in the case, are distributed among the audience. All the papers have been prefolded, then opened out so that when refolded, they will seem identical.

The volunteer who selects one of the folded papers bearing the name of a playing card passes it to the mentalist. The mentalist holds the prepared cardcase with his right thumb over the indentation in the box and his fingers at the back of the box. Receiving the folded paper in his left hand, he places it on the case so that it comes slightly under the right thumb.

Raising his right hand to display the paper and the cardboard case, he says, "Many people wrote down the name of a playing card. One piece of paper has been selected by a volunteer. On it is the name of a card in this pack. Neither I nor anyone else here knows which card has been chosen."

The magician puts the case, front side down, on the palm of his left hand, and gives the paper to the volunteer. At least he seems to give the paper to the volunteer. The moment the case rests on the palm of his left hand, he slides the hidden slip of paper away from the indentation with his right hand and, taking it up between thumb and fingers, it is this he gives to the volunteer. The case now covers the slip originally selected by the volunteer as it rests on the mentalist's palm.

This is a very deceptive move. As the thumb presses against the concealed paper, the thumb can effortlessly draw it away. There is no clue to even the closest observer of any other piece of paper. It looks as if the mentalist had simply placed the case in his obviously empty left hand, and with his right hand, passed the square of paper to the spectator.

With his right thumb, the mentalist opens the cover and

removes the pack of cards. The empty box is dropped into his left-hand coat pocket along with the original paper.

"Open the paper and make a mental picture of the card," the mentalist tells the spectator. The mentalist then goes through the pack, and takes out the card whose name he himself has earlier scrawled on the paper.

THINK OF A DISTANT CITY

"Think of a faraway city," the mentalist tells the audience, "one you have visited or one you would like to see. It can be in Asia, Europe, Australia, or North or South America. Then call out the name."

As the cities are mentioned, the mentalist writes down each name, one by one, on pieces of paper, which he crumples and drops on the table.

After fifteen or more cities have been called out, the mentalist asks a spectator to mix the papers and choose one. Then the mentalist unrolls a map of the world, which he holds in his left hand.

"I will look at the map as you turn your back, open the paper you have chosen, and think about the selected city. Once you have the name of the city fixed in your mind, let me know, but don't call out the name."

Eventually the spectator says he or she is concentrating on the city.

The mentalist asks several questions: "Have you ever been to this place?" "Would you like to travel there?" "Can you visualize the continent in which it is located?" He moves his right index finger from continent to continent across the map, then stops on one particular one. "Correct?" As the spectator concentrates on the country, the magician similarly moves his finger, then again brings it to rest. "Right?" Receiving affirmative answers to these questions, he asks the spectator to form a mental picture of the city. As the spectator does so, the mentalist describes, then dramatically identifies the chosen city.

Before the performance, the mentalist has written Paris on twenty two-inch squares of paper; that is, unless the show is taking place in Paris, in which case Rome or London would be a better choice. He holds the papers written side down in his left hand as he seemingly writes down the names provided by the audience. Actually the performer uses a ball point pen with the tip retracted. Though he goes through the motions of writing, no marks are made on the squares of paper. Each square is crumpled by squeezing it between the thumb and forefingers so that the name previously written on the lower side is brought to the center of the crumpled ball.

Since Paris has been put on all the squares of papers, this will inevitably be the chosen city. If, by the time the names of seventeen cities have been called, Paris has not been included, pretend that you heard someone say Paris. (I have never had to do this, but it is only fair I tell you how to meet such an emergency.)

It isn't really necessary to have a map of the world. You can present the mental demonstration without it, though the map adds visual interest.

THINK OF A BALL PLAYER . . .

You can, if you prefer, use the same method to divine the name of a selected World Series pitcher, international soccer star, television host, or best-selling author. In each of these fields, there is at least one name that will always be mentioned when twenty are listed.

You can also have the names of various objects called out, but those of famous people or exotic places are more interesting. As each name is called, you tell the audience something about the object or the personality as you write.

At election time, presidential candidates make a logical category. Some of the politicians' names will arouse emotion when they are heard. Legendary villains may provoke similar responses from the audience.

FORGERY WHILE BLINDFOLDED

Many performers while blindfolded describe the clothes worn by members of the audience, identify objects held by onlookers, and read from a book or magazine opened at any page. Dr. Stanley Jaks had a different approach. He duplicated signatures —writing upside down and backward.

He prefaced this demonstration by showing placards bearing the autographs of several prominent people and pointing out that the signatures reflected the characteristics of the signers. For instance, film star Jane Russell's autograph suggested her physical attractions, and aircraft designer Alexander de Seversky's was reminiscent of the lines of his planes and his streamlined thinking.

Rather than a complicated blindfold, Jaks preferred one that was simple yet convincing. Round sponge-rubber makeup pads were placed over each closed eye, then a wide, black opaque blindfold was put over the pads and tied at the back of his head.

He was led behind a chair. Tilted up from the seat to the back of the chair was a large oblong piece of cardboard. Below a horizontal line, dividing the front surface of the cardboard in half, a spectator had written his or her signature with a wide-tipped felt pen.

Reaching down to let his hand pass over the cardboard, apparently to "see" the upside-down signature with his fingers without actually touching it, Jaks swiftly wrote backward, above the dividing line, an exact forgery of the autograph.

As with other blindfolded performers, Jaks saw with his eyes, not his fingers. By opening his eyes and raising his brow, he was able to move up the pads and the blindfold slightly.

Looking down the sides of his nose, he could see the name. He had studied art in Europe and was skillful with a pen. He told me it was far easier to duplicate a signature when it was upside down; then it appeared to be an irregular pattern.

One of his most interesting close-up mysteries was the signature duplication on a smaller scale. When we had lunch soon after he came to the United States from Switzerland, Jaks drew a line across the back of a small white card and had me write beneath the line. Sliding the card across the table without reversing it, he quickly reproduced my signature. This upside-down writing, he commented, was a trick used by forgers.

If you have artistic talent, you can present either Jaks's intimate version of this feat or the stage variation with a blindfold. Lacking this ability, you can duplicate words members of your audience have printed, writing them upside down and backward, while wearing a blindfold and leaning forward over a large piece of cardboard.

DESIGN PROJECTION

Years ago during an engagement in a hotel in the Bahamas, I introduced a novel way to duplicate geometric designs drawn by spectators. Before being blindfolded, I gave a piece of chalk and a sixteen-inch square of thick black cardboard to each of four volunteers. After my eyes were blindfolded, I told the volunteers to stand to my left and draw any geometric figure they wished on their pieces of cardboard without showing it to any other members of the audience.

I extended my left hand for the first piece of cardboard, which had its blank side turned toward the front. Holding the square about thigh high and raising my right hand to touch my forehead above the blindfold, I could look down and see the back of the cardboard—and the design—while I told the volunteer artist to mentally project an image of the figure.

Holding the board higher with the blank side still to the front, I drew on that side a similar design. As soon as the work was completed, I turned the card around so the audience could compare the two drawings. Then I repeated the feat with the three other designs.

After a few nights, I decided to have the fourth volunteer print a word. This variation gave a stronger finish to the routine.

Soft chalk produces bolder lines than hard chalk, and thick pieces produce wider lines; wide sticks of soft chalk are recommended for stage performances.

One more thought about blindfolds: If the feats you perform while wearing them are intended to simulate demonstrations of clairvoyance, keep your eyes closed until you peek, and walk cautiously as if you really are unable to see. If, however, you are exhibiting what seems to be eyeless vision, keep your eyes open and move boldly about.

An example of the eyeless-vision approach is to describe an object placed in your hand when it is held about waist high. If you can get a peek at the object before it is placed in your hand, ask the person who has it to hold it behind your back; then you apparently can see with the back of your head as well as with your fingertips.

THE PREDESTINED NUMBER

"I wrote a prediction this morning," the mentalist says as he slips a sealed envelope under an ashtray in a living room. He gives a spectator a pack of cards, then turns away. "Please shuffle the cards and let me know when they are thoroughly mixed."

Upon being assured that the shuffle has been completed, the mentalist continues, "Divide the pack into two piles of about the same size on the table." He pauses. "Turn several cards face-up on the left-hand pile—say less than ten to save time." He pauses again. "Turn the same number of cards face-up on the right-hand pile." After a third pause, he says, "Put the left-hand pile on top of the right-hand pile, then give the pack to me behind my back."

When this has been done, the mentalist swings around to face the spectator. "This morning I did not know how many cards you would choose," he continues, "but I felt certain that if I, too, turned some up, I would be able to predict the total number face-up in this pack." He brings the cards forward.

"Remember, you shuffled the cards, and I did not see what happened once I turned away. Please count the number of face-up cards." The moment the total is announced, the performer points to the envelope. "Tear it open and read my predicition." The prediction is correct.

This feat can be performed with a borrowed pack. You can vary your predcition each time you do the trick. Suppose you write twenty. When the pack is behind your back, silently count off twenty cards from the top of the pack and turn them upside down. If you write nineteen beforehand, turn nineteen face-down.

You do not know, nor do you need to know, the number of cards the spectator turns face-up. Yet the impression is given that you divined this number.

Sealing your prophecy in an envelope and putting the envelope under the ashtray at the start of the trick diverts attention from the simple mathematical formula that makes the marvel possible.

SEEING THROUGH METAL

A spectator examines a metal file-card case. He lifts the hinged top. In the box are six small rubber balls of different colors. He is told to take all of the balls except one and drop them into his side coat pocket. He is to remember the color of the ball in the box. After he closes the lid, he is to snap a rubber band around the box to keep the top firmly closed. This is done while the performer has his back turned or goes into another room.

The mentalist asks no questions. He picks up the file-card case and says, "The interior is dark. Even if I could see through solid metal, I would not be able to make out the color of the ball in the box. So I must visualize you removing five balls." He pauses. "Green, blue, yellow, brown, and orange. That leaves but one. It is red."

A standard green metal file-card box is used. It is 3⅜ inches high, 5¼ inches long, and 3¼ inches wide. The hinged lid is 1½ inches deep. Neither the box nor the six rubber balls are prepared.

After the spectator has followed your instructions, take the box in your right hand, fingers at the back, thumb on the front of the lid to the right, as shown in the illustration.

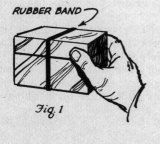

RUBBER BAND

Fig. 1

Fig. 2

As you talk, tilt the box slightly away from you. The rubber ball will roll noiselessly across the bottom of the box to the side that is hinged at the top. With a light upward push of your thumb on the front of the lid, you can open the lid just enough to glance inside. Don't look at the box. Look at the spectator. Lift the box and touch it to your forehead. As the slight opening passes your eyes, you can see the color of the ball inside—if there is a light in the room that shines in the box from above or behind you.

In a well-lighted room or on a stage you should have no trouble peering through the narrow opening. Close the box as it touches your forehead.

The rubber band around the file-card case stretches imperceptibly as the lid is opened.

Don't say the color of the ball immediately. Place the box on a table and direct your attention to the spectator as you build to the climax.

FOR A SINGLE SPECTATOR

When I first presented this for a single seated spectator, I lifted the box from the table where she had placed it and held it momentarily to her forehead. During the upward passage of the box, I raised the lid for a glimpse, then sighted the ball as the box touched her forehead. Later I found that the box could be opened secretly without any risk of detection even when there were onlookers on three sides.

Hold the box between your hands with your palms at the sides and your fingers at the back. Press on the lid to hold it level, then let the box drop slightly at the hinge. You can easily open the box half an inch, and yet have the angles covered. Only a ⅛-inch gap is necessary to see the ball. With a larger opening, you can identify playing cards or ESP cards that have been put face-up in the box.

URI GELLER'S HANDLING

I have seen films of Uri Geller, who claims to have extraordinary extrasensory powers, demonstrating his skill by predicting what number would be uppermost on a die after it has been shaken in a file-card case. Parapsychologists were astonished by this exhibition of a seemingly supernatural gift.

I was less impressed. The movements Geller used to peek in the box as he held it were the very ones I had described in an article in *Hugard's Magic Monthly* in September 1963. This was long before Uri began his career as a psychic.

GELLER'S WATCH TRICK

Perhaps the best of Geller's tricks technically is the one he presents with a borrowed wristwatch. He notes the time and puts the watch, dial side down, on the palm of the volunteer's hand; he then tells the volunteer to close his or her fingers.

Uri clenches his fist above the closed hand and seems to strain. When the volunteer looks at the face of the watch, the hands indicate that hours have passed in less than a minute.

"The hands moved while I held the watch. He didn't touch it," guillible volunteers say, forgetting that it was Geller who had placed the watch on the palm of their hands.

You can perform this trick yourself. Hold the watch face-up, the stem turned toward your palm, resting on the inner sides of your middle and ring fingers, with the strap dangling down between your ring and little fingers on one side and between your index and middle fingers on the other.

Extend your open hand to show the time on the watch. Ask the volunteer to hold out his or her right hand with the palm face-up. Your eyes go from the volunteer's eyes to the volunteer's hand.

The moment the volunteer's hand is extended, your right hand turns so that its back is turned to the front. Your right thumbnail, hidden from view, pulls out the stem of the watch. With short quick rolls of the ball of your thumb, you then advance the time.

As you raise your hand to put the watch face-down in the volunteer's palm, move your thumb aside and squeeze the watch between your fingers and palm. This pushes the stem back into place.

When the watch is face-down on the owner's palm, neither the volunteer nor other spectators can see that the time has been advanced.

You can if you wish squeeze your fist over his or her closed hand as Geller does, but please don't claim that you have uncanny powers from outer space.

CONCENTRATE ON A COLOR

Holding a large pad in one hand and a felt-tipped pen in the other, the mentalist stands at the front of the stage and asks a volunteer, whom he has directed to stand several feet behind him, to select one of six 14-inch squares of heavy cardboard of different colors.

"Choose one of the squares. Hold it up, then concentrate on the color," the mentalist directs. "Think only of the color. Visualize it in your mind."

The mentalist attempts to receive the thought. Suddenly he prints something on his pad, then swings the pad around so that the audience can see what he has written. It is the name of the color.

Few feats of mentalism are so simple—or so baffling. Less ingenious performers sometimes have a confederate seated near the front, who, by movements of the head or other visual signals, conveys the required data.

In this feat, the mentalist works alone. Hidden by the fingers that grasp the pen is a small mirror. As the mentalist wrinkles his brow, he raises the hand that holds the pen. With the mirror properly positioned, he can see in it a reflection of the colored card.

Why doesn't the spectator who has chosen the color see the mirror? When the mentalist gives his instructions, he tells the spectator to close his or her eyes and mentally visualize the color. The glimpse is made a moment later.

SUPER PSYCHOMETRY

"Psychometry is the art of sensing information from an object," the mentalist explains. "A bloodhound can track down a shirt's owner. A psychometrist can stand in an ancient temple and visualize the people who once carried out rites within its walls. If six volunteers will come to the stage, I will try an unusual experiment."

The six volunteers upon their arrival are seated side by side in a row of chairs and each is given an envelope. After the mentalist has been blindfolded, they seal personal articles—a watch, key, coin, pen, or whatever they choose—in the six opaque envelopes.

One of the volunteers then collects the envelopes, mixes them up so that no one can know to whom they belong, then gives them one by one to the blindfolded mentalist. The aim of the performer is not to name the objects but to give a graphic description of their owners.

"I get the impression of a thin man, more than six feet tall," the mentalist begins as he holds the first envelope. "This man has a small scar on his left cheek." The mentalist rips open the envelope and takes from it a key. "Will the person who put this key in the envelope claim his property?" A lean, lanky man with a scar on the left side of his face takes the key.

Holding another envelope, the mentalist says, "I see a woman with blonde hair. She likes to read, but sometimes has difficulty in making out the small print." He removes a pen from the envelope. A woman with straw-colored hair, wearing glasses, comes forward for her pen.

The owners of the objects in the other four envelopes are described just as accurately.

For this feat, the mentalist must have a good memory. He must remember the appearances of the people who come up to assist him. As he distributes the envelopes, he notes the seat each person occupies. The envelopes are secretly marked so they can be identified solely by touch. The marks are made near the right edge of the flap sides. The uppermost will signal that it came from the volunteer seated in the first chair. The next, marked half an inch below, will bring to mind the person in the second chair, and so on.

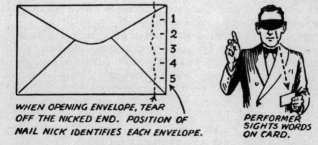

WHEN OPENING ENVELOPE, TEAR OFF THE NICKED END. POSITION OF NAIL NICK IDENTIFIES EACH ENVELOPE.

PERFORMER SIGHTS WORDS ON CARD.

The marks if carefully made will not be observed by the participants. They are merely slight indentations formed by grasping an envelope between thumb and index finger and pressing down with the thumbnail on one side as the tip of the index finger squeezes on the other.

During the performance the mentalist holds each envelope between his thumb and fingers. By touch alone, he knows which of the six people is involved.

If by chance a credit card, social security card, or a membership card bearing the owner's name is put into an envelope, the performer, peering down from the blindfold, can read the name as he removes the card. After the owner claims the card, the mentalist can add a demonstration of thought-reading to the routine. He asks the card's owner to think of his or her name; then the performer calls out the name.

SHOE CLUE

Sight, not touch, and memory are the keys to this extemporaneous version of psychometry. The mentalist must remember not only the appearance of the people who participate but the differences in their shoes.

A borrowed scarf or a large handkerchief serves as a blindfold. Close your eyes securely as the blindfold is being applied.

Invite the participants to come forward one at a time. Extend the open palm of your left hand holding it about waist high and ten inches out from your body. Tell the first volunteer to place a personal object in your hand. As you talk, tilt your head forward, open your eyes, raise your brow, and in so doing, move up the blindfold slightly.

Peering down, you will then be able to catch sight of the shoes. Raise your hand to the level of the blindfold. Describe the sex, height, weight, and other details you have associated in your mind with the wearer of the shoes.

Repeat this procedure with each of the other participants.

Acting ability is more essential than digital dexterity to the mentalist. A good actor will make even the simplest feat appear very difficult. He will seem to struggle at times to receive projected thoughts, to get mental impressions. He will also add humor to break the tension after a dramatic feat. Acknowledging the applause, he might say, "Now if only I can remember where I parked my car tonight," or "That's really much easier to do than filling out the new income-tax forms."

Milbourne Christopher and Garry Moore try a feat of mental magic before the telecast of The World's Greatest Magicians.

Two-Person Telepathy

Perhaps at some time in the remote future, telephones will become obsolete, and we will send messages just by thinking about them. This will undoubtedly produce red faces and provoke fights on occasion. If you think the air waves are cluttered now, just imagine the chaos that could be created by millions of people attempting to direct their thoughts to the proper destination. Thought static will certainly be more nervewracking than radio static. Politicians will no longer have secrets, and intelligence-gathering agencies will be surfeited with unwanted data.

At the moment, despite the high hopes of parapsychologists, no two people have yet been found who can consistently communicate even simple words without error—by the mind alone, that is. There are now, and there have been in the past, many performers who create the illusion that they are able to send and receive thoughts.

Some have developed diabolically clever codes, both oral and unspoken. With movements of the eyes and positions of the head, a good sender can transmit names, social-security numbers, and foreign words with no obvious actions that someone not familiar with the method can detect.

Many spoken codes are complicated and hard to master. The one I am about to describe can be learned with little effort. One of the strong points in its favor is that the words are not spoken by the sender to the receiver, but are addressed to a spectator.

CARD IMAGERY

This seeming demonstration of extrasensory perception can be performed equally well in a living room or on a stage. After the performer's female assistant has been securely blindfolded, a member of the audience is asked to shuffle a pack of cards. The performer then fans the cards or spreads them out face-up and invites the volunteer to select one and make a mental image of it. Soon the blindfolded receiver identifies the card.

If the chosen card is a diamond, the performer points at it, looks at the volunteer, and inquires, "This?" If it is a club, the performer asks, "This one?" A heart is indicated by, "This one here?" Nothing is said if the card is a spade. In other words, one word for diamonds; two words for clubs; three words for hearts; silence for spades.

Continuing his conversation with the volunteer, the performer tells her or him to "Think," "Now think," "Think of it," or "Now think of it."

There are thirteen cards in each suit. One word is used to indicate that the card is an ace, deuce, or trey; two words are used for a four, five, or six; three words, for a seven, eight, or nine; four words, for a ten, jack, or queen; silence, for a king.

The final cue, addressed like the others to the person who is thinking of the card, is not sent until the blindfolded assistant has finished giving her initial impression. The assistant may say if the card signaled is a spade that she seems to perceive a coal mine and miners working in it with tools, thus specifying the suit of spades. The other suits are then described with similar suitable imagery.

As soon as the assistant mentions a suit, the performer turns to the spectator for verification, asking either "Right?" or "That's right?" or "Is that right?" One word indicates the first card of the previously signaled group. Two words specify the second card, and three words, the third card.

The blindfolded assistant now knows the exact card and describes it as interestingly as she can. Obviously when a king is the selected card, the third cue is unnecessary.

The basic idea for this code was devised by my friend Orville Meyer. In his presentation, the performer talks directly to the blindfolded assistant. I have found it more effective to address my remarks to the person who selected the card.

COLOR CODE

The same cue structure can be used to cue colors. Print the following colors on a sheet of paper if you are going to perform in a living room. Use a large piece of cardboard on the stage.

RED	BLACK
WHITE	PURPLE
BLUE	SILVER
YELLOW	GOLD
GREEN	BROWN
ORANGE	GRAY

The performer reads off the colors, then approaches a member of the audience. "Please touch one," he says, "and think of the color." The performer, to confirm the choice, inquires, "This?" "This one?" "This one here?" or remains silent.

One word signals the first group of three—red, white, or blue; two words, the second group—yellow, green, or orange; and so on. You may have noticed that the colors are grouped so that they are easy to remember.

Then, as in the card system, the performer instructs the spectator to "Think," "Now think," or "Think of it."

No further cue is required. If the blindfolded assistant has heard a single word spoken at the start, then two words spoken later, she realizes she can describe a winter scene in words of this nature: "It's bitter cold. I see a cabin among trees. Smoke curls from a chimney. There are tracks in the snow leading to the door of the cabin. Snow? Yes, snow is the dominant feature of the landscape. It is piled high around the cabin, and at the bases of the trees. . . . The color is white!"

One word, then three words could trigger: "I see a speed boat racing across an expanse of water. People are cheering; it's a race. The sun is shining; the sky is clear. I know this area. It's near Bermuda. The sky is blue and the water seems to be blue, too. That's the color—blue."

Three words plus two might inspire: "I see a color-television screen. A special event is being telecast. I hear stirring music, and see many uniforms. There is a golden carriage drawn by white horses. A liveried attendant opens the door. The queen in royal regalia is leaving the carriage. The color? Is it the red of the uniforms? The gold of crown and carriage? No! It is the rich purple of her robe."

Simply to name the color is not enough. The words preceding the revelation must add drama and excitement to the presentation.

PRESIDENTIAL CHOICE

Another variation affords the blindfolded receiver the opportunity to impress the audience with her knowledge of American history. The names of twelve Presidents are lettered on a placard.

WASHINGTON	ROOSEVELT
JEFFERSON	EISENHOWER
ADAMS	TRUMAN
LINCOLN	KENNEDY
TAFT	FORD
COOLIDGE	CARTER

The ability of the assistant to graphically depict an incident in the chosen Chief Executive's life and then to describe his appearance enhances the feat.

TUNE TELEPATHY

Perhaps the most puzzling and certainly the most lively application of this code is designed for a theatre. A cooperative pianist, who is a member of the theatre's orchestra, aids the performer.

The performer invites the audience to call out the names of twelve popular songs. As each of them is suggested, the performer lists the name of the song on a pad. A member of the audience comes to the stage to select a tune mentally.

After making his or her decision, the volunteer whispers the title to the performer so that only he can hear. He touches the pad and asks, "This?" "This one?" "This one here?" or remains silent.

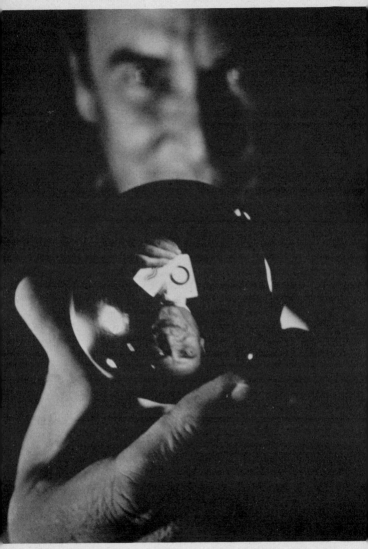

Philippe Halsman took this curious photograph. Note that Christopher's face is reflected and distorted in the crystal ball.

Then he tells the spectator to "Think," "Now think," "Think of it," or "Now think of it." As he or she concentrates, the orchestra plays the melody.

Before the show, the performer rehearses privately with the pianist. The pianist is given a sheet of music. On it is space for the musician to jot down the tunes as they are called. The simple code is explained, then practiced with any twelve tunes that come to mind.

During the performance, as the performer writes down the names of the songs on a pad, the musician makes note of them, too. After hearing the second spoken cue, the pianist begins playing and the other members of the orchestra join in. Ask the piano player not to reveal the secret to the other musicians. They will think he or she has unusual ESP powers.

TELEPHONE TELEPATHY

While talking at a party, turn the conversation to telepathy. Say you have been experimenting with a friend and have achieved remarkable results. If the other guests are interested, phone your assistant, and ask if she would mind participating in a test. When the assistant expresses approval, borrow a pack of cards. Have it shuffled, then proceed as the assistant listens. With the spoken cues, the assistant can name the card even if she is in another city.

This presentation is also impressive if you are in a newspaper columnist's office or are a guest on a radio talk show. In the latter case, you can also use the following method to convey the name of a chosen card.

THE TELLTALE VOICE

Have a person shuffle a pack of cards, and cut the pack into two nearly equal piles. Have the person then choose one of the piles. Spread those cards face-down between your hands and ask the person to take a card, remember it, and replace it.

Turn your back, then tell your subject to write down the name of the card on a piece of paper, fold the paper in half, and hide the paper.

"Keep one card in mind," Christopher suggests, and Rodin's "Thinker" seems to ponder and concentrate on his choice. (Photograph by Sodelvia Pickard)

"Would you be surprised if someone you never met, someone who is at this moment in another city, told you the name of the card?" you ask.

Give the subject a long-distance telephone number to call. When the phone call is answered, a voice says, "You are thinking of a playing card. I have developed a talent similar to the one employed by lie-detector technicians. Pick up the pile of cards with your card in it. Turn the cards face-up and read off their names, one at a time, pronouncing each word as distinctly as you can."

The subject follows these instructions; then the voice in another city names the card.

Perhaps the most interesting angle to this presentation is that your assistant does not know which card has been chosen until the subject says its name.

The method is bold yet simple. As you extend the cards for the selection to be made, you silently count down nine cards from the top. When the subject is ready to replace the card, lift off the nine cards as you divide the pile and drop them on top of the chosen one.

Square up the cards before you put them down. Misdirect the subject's attention by asking him or her to write down the name of the card. Your assistant is, of course, aware that the tenth card mentioned by the subject will be the selected one.

After the assistant names it, ask to see the name of the card written on the piece of paper, so that you can verify the long-distance statement.

Note that I specified that only half a pack is to be employed in this feat. It takes too long to call out fifty-two cards. Tension will diminish.

There is always the very remote possibility that your assistant may develop genuine telepathic ability. If so, call the most important psychic researchers and the principal newspapers immediately. Anyone who can perform this and the previous feats without trickery is bound to become an overnight celebrity!

A mentalist creates the illusion that he can send and receive thoughts. Acting ability is even more important than technical skill.

Book Tests

The morning before I was to lecture on new developments in conjuring for the Academy of Magical Arts in Hollywood, I was thumbing through a copy of *TV Guide* and accidentally made a discovery that led to a new version of a book test.

Book tests are frequently presented by mentalists. The illusion is created that a performer reads a spectator's thoughts while he or she is thinking of one or more words on a printed page. Many methods have been devised to produce this effect. Some require ingeniously prepared books or magazines; others can be presented only under certain conditions.

PSYCHIC VISION

I have in my collection a book of poetry once owned by an alleged psychic. A client could open this book at any page, read several verses silently, then close the volume, and give it to the charlatan when he came into the room. Soon the charlatan could recite the words himself—if, that is, the conditions were favorable.

It was necessary for the client to read the verses by the light of a table lamp and for the trickster to open the volume in a dark area of the room. Otherwise, his "powers" would fail. A minute dot of luminous paint was on every page of the book. The dots normally could not be seen. A bright light activated the luminous material. Once the book was in the shadow, the charlatan had only to turn the pages until he came to one with a glowing speck. This indicated where the book had been opened by the client.

The feat I worked out in Hollywood is presented with an unprepared magazine and can be shown under almost every conceivable circumstance.

TELETHOUGHT

The mentalist asks a spectator to examine the current issue of *TV Guide,* then to bring it to the platform. Standing to the left of the volunteer from the audience, the performer says, "I will turn away my head and flick through the pages. Call out, 'Stop,' whenever you wish." The pages fly by before the spectator can speak. "Too quick?" the performer asks. "Let's try again." This time the pace is slower. The moment the spectator calls, "Stop," the magazine is opened at this point and given to him.

Without even glancing at the magazine, the mentalist walks several feet away. Standing with his back to the spectator, he says, "Look at the page on your left. *Silently* read whatever is there. If, by chance, there is an advertisement on the page, make a mental picture of it. If it's a series of program listings, remember the name of the first few shows and something about them."

As this is being done, the mentalist addresses the audience: "If sharp mental images are projected, and if I can receive them clearly, you are about to see a remarkable demonstration. I may fail, but I'll do my best." The performer tells the volunteer to close the magazine, then swings around to face him.

"Ready? Concentrate!" Seeming to strain to get a mental impression, the mentalist closes his eyes. "A comedy program. Yes, I see the leading characters." He gives their names and recalls a funny incident from an episode in the show. Then he pauses. "Now you are thinking about a sports event." He identifies the sport and the opposing teams. The mentalist opens his eyes. "Am I right?" The spectator acknowledges that he is.

Stapled at the center of the magazine as issued is an advertising section printed on heavier paper than the other pages. Hold the spine in your right hand, bend the pages to the left with the ball of your left thumb on the back cover. Let the pages fly by your thumb, and by touch alone you will be able to locate the center pages. After flipping through the pages rapidly the first time, start to riffle them again. Whenever the spectator calls, "Stop," pull down quickly with your thumb. The magazine will open with program listings to the left and the first heavier page of the advertising section to the right.

The initial rapid run-through of the pages has a dual purpose. It alerts the spectator to the fact that he must speak almost at once, and it produces a laugh from the audience.

Before performing, commit the first few listings on the left-hand page to memory. You can then display the feat with any one of the millions of copies of that issue.

Remember to instruct the spectator as he looks at the open magazine while your back is turned to read silently. Otherwise the volunteer may read the words aloud and spoil your trick.

Other magazines have similar advertising inserts printed on heavier stock, and I have seen several paperback novels that carry them. You might wish to experiment with some of these.

The revelation of the spectator's thoughts should be presented with as much drama as possible. As you know in advance what will be on the "freely selected" page, rehearse what you will say, choosing your words with care.

PAPERBACK BOOK TEST

Long before introducing Telethought, I presented a similar mystery with a paperback book. I had found that when a straight pin was thrust through the spine of a paperback and pushed in completely, the pages when riffled by the thumb would open to those adjacent to the pin. After memorizing the first few words on the left-hand page, I could reveal a spectator's thoughts as described in the previous presentation.

The best books to manipulate are those that have from 150 to 250 pages. The pages must be numbered at the top, not at the bottom. The mentalist's head is turned to the left as he asks a volunteer, placed at his right, to concentrate on a number he sees as the pages fly by.

Flick through the pages quickly, too quickly for a number to be seen until you reach the two pages between which the pin is lodged. The pin will cause just enough of a pause for the spectator to sight the number at the top of the left-hand page before the remaining pages whisk rapidly by.

Close the book, then walk a few feet away. Explain that the spectator is to open the book to the chosen page and fix the first several words of the top line in his mind. As you talk, slip your thumbnail under the head of the pin and pull the pin out.

Give the book to the spectator, stand with your back turned toward the other person, put your hands in your pockets, and get rid of the pin. Allow the spectator time to concentrate on the words before you begin spelling them out. You may wonder why the spectator does not see the pin when the pages are riffled. Being only partially opened, the pages conceal the pin. Also, since his attention was directed to the page numbers, the spectator's eyes are focused at the top.

FOUR-BOOK VARIATION

Memorize the first three words in the first sentences of three books with different titles on whatever page you decide to use and prepare in a fourth volume with the method described above. Toss the three unprepared books to as many spectators in various parts of the audience. Toss the fourth book, the one with the pin, to someone seated in the first or second row. As soon as the last person catches the book, ask him to bring it to the stage.

As before, spell out the words in the spectator's mind, then ask him to announce the number of the page. Ask the three members of the audience having books to stand and open their books to the selected page.

Reveal the words they think of in the first lines of their pages. As you know the order of the books, start with the first three words you have memorized, then the second three, and finally the third. Act as though it were difficult to discern the words. Pause between them to build up suspense.

If you prefer to give a shorter demonstration, toss out three

When the performer is blindfolded before a mental feat, this adds to the astonishment provoked by the seemingly impossible demonstration.

books rather than four. The fact that people in the audience have had an opportunity to examine the books they receive adds to the impact of the mystery.

An occasional spectator may think that you memorized the first lines on every page of each book. If he voices this suspicion later, point out that this would involve committing to memory many hundreds of words—no small feat—and that you did not know which page would be selected.

NOVEL TELEPATHY

The ease with which the mentalist acquires the vital secret data in this book test permits him to devote most of his effort to putting the feat across.

As the audience sees it, three spectators take books, examine them, then decide what page, line, and word they each will choose. As the first spectator thinks of the selected word, the mentalist writes something on an 8- by 10-inch—or even larger —piece of cardboard. Then, without showing what he has written, he inserts the cardboard into an envelope, and gives this to the first spectator. This procedure is repeated with the two other participants.

The three spectators are told to print the words they chose in large letters with a broad-tipped felt pen on the back of their envelopes, concealing the words from the audience as they do so.

Summing up what has gone before, the mentalist tells the first spectator to read aloud his word and show it to the audience, then remove the piece of cardboard from the envelope. The mentalist now takes the cardboard and emphasizes that the word he wrote earlier is the very same word that the spectator chose. The words in the two remaining envelopes prove also to match those written by the other two spectators.

At this point you may be thinking that the words were transferred by carbon paper when the spectators wrote on the envelopes. This, however, is not the case. The mentalist's three words are written in longhand, the spectators' printed in block letters.

Needed for this feat are four novels, either clothbound or paperback. Three of the books are unprepared, the fourth is doctored in a way that will be described shortly. Three pieces of white cardboard, as many envelopes, and four felt-tipped pens also play a part in the deception.

To prepare for this feat, sit at a table. Open three books to page 1. A long ruler placed across the pages when the open books are set side by side will hold them in position for quick reference.

Turn to page 1 of the fourth book. With a short horizontal stroke of your pen, divide the white space in the left margin in half. Swing the book to the left. Write the first words of the other three books in sequence to the left of the dividing mark. To the right of it, inscribe the first words of the three books' last lines.

Turn all the books to page 2. This time divide the right margin of the fourth book in half. Write the first three cue words to the left of the mark and the last three cue words to the right. Continue this process until you have coded every page in all three books. The secret data will as a result be in the left margins of the odd-number pages and in the right margins of the even-numbered pages.

A guidebook prepared as described will conceal the secret information in an unusual way. You can open the pages—as long as you don't open them too widely—without the writing in the inner margins being seen. Once prepared, such a set of four books can be used for years.

Select books with distinctive covers, so you can tell one from another at a glance. For example, let's say the first book has a red jacket; the second, a yellow wrapper; the third, a green cover; and the fourth, which is to be your guide, is blue.

To aid in getting the correct words quickly, think of the red book as one, the yellow as two, and the green as three. Before your show, stack the books in this order: red at the top; yellow, green, and blue at the bottom. Should someone backstage pick up a book and open it, it is not likely that such a person will take the bottom book. The upper three, of course, are unprepared.

During the performance, pick up the stack, and give the top book to the volunteer on the left, the second book to the person next to him, and the third book to the spectator at the right. Retain the guidebook. Use it to illustrate what the volunteers are to do. Flick through the pages as you invite the participants to examine their books and compare one with another.

Two volunteers are involved in the choices of pages and lines. The first calls out a number between 1 and 250. All are told to open their books to this page. You open your book to show how this is done. The second volunteer makes a selection of either the first or last line. Point to your partially opened page to indicate that they must concentrate on the first word of the chosen line.

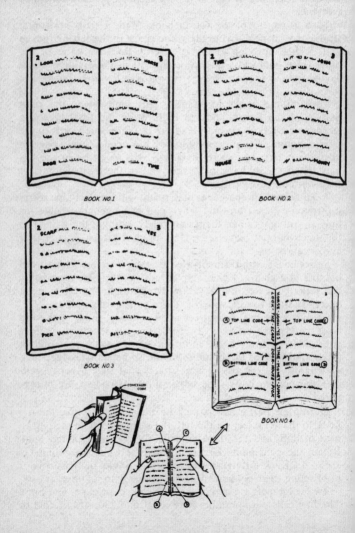

Open your own book wider and, glancing at the three words in the proper portion of the margin, memorize them.

Close your book, put it on the table, and pick up one of the pieces of cardboard and a pen. Ask the first spectator to concentrate on the chosen word; as he or she does so, write on the cardboard the first of the three words you saw in the margin. Without showing the word, slip the cardboard into an envelope. Give this envelope and a pen to the first spectator, taking away the closed book as you do so.

Repeat these actions, while you seem to be reading the thoughts of the other spectators and exchanging the envelopes containing your written words for their books.

Tell the participants to print the words they were to think of on the backs of their envelopes. While they are busy following your instructions, address the audience:

"These three people, whom I have never before met, came to the stage to assist me. They selected the page number, line, and word the three of them were to think of from as many different books. I then wrote down what I thought the three of them were thinking. I may not be completely correct. If I have succeeded in getting only *one* of the words, I think you will agree with me, this is a remarkable achievement."

Turn to the first spectator. "Will you, please, tell the audience your word and show what you have written."

Pause a few seconds; then reach into the first envelope, and pull out the cardboard. "Earlier I received and wrote this word." Display it.

After the second volunteer has named and shown his word, pull out the second cardboard so the audience can see that you've scored a second hit.

"Two out of three; now for the third word." Smile as the third spectator says his or her word and turns the envelope so that the writing on it is visible to the audience. Reach confidently into the envelope. Withdraw the cardboard with a flourish.

This feat builds to an applause-producing climax. It may be presented on the largest stage. I am indebted to my friend Hen Fetsch for the concept.

Garry Moore mentally pictured Steve Allen during this I've Got a Secret *telecast. A wave of Christopher's hand produced Allen by Moore's side.*

ONE WORD AMONG THOUSANDS

The previous routine required extensive preparation. This one is presented extemporaneously—with a borrowed book. There's one qualification. The numbers must be printed at the top of the pages and, preferably, at the side rather than in the center.

Standing beside a volunteer selected from the audience, the mentalist asks the spectator to select and remember the number of any one page as the performer riffles through a book.

"Do you have it in mind?" the mentalist asks. If so, he gives the closed book to the volunteer; if not, he riffles through the book again. Once the performer has presented the closed book to the spectator, he strides to the far side of the stage.

"Open the book to the number you selected. Think of the first word of the first line of that page; then close the book," the mentalist continues, keeping his face turned away.

As the spectator concentrates on the word, the mentalist spells it out correctly.

Considerable practice is needed to present this book test perfectly. Once you have acquired the skill, you can perform at a moment's notice.

You must learn how to make the pages fly past the ball of your thumb, so that only a single page number can be seen. Somewhere about the center of the book, as the pages flick rapidly by, there is a very slight pause; then the other pages go by just as rapidly as their predecessors. The spectator's eyes have been directed to the numbers. Your attention is focused on the first words on the pages. You do not see the number he remembers; he is not aware of the word you memorize.

Once you have mastered this quick-glimpse technique, you can spot the first word of the second, third, or fourth line instead of the first—or the first word of the last line.

When a paperback book is used, hold the volume between the thumb and fingers of your left hand, bend the pages to the right, and let them spring past the ball of your right thumb. With a hardback book, after opening the cover, grasp the pages with your right hand for the riffling process.

This book test is as practical for a single spectator in an office, as it is for performance onstage before a large audience.

To insure that the word you are about to reveal is the right one, there's a bit of byplay that will give you a clue. Ask the spectator to concentrate on the word and tap his right index finger on the palm of his left hand as he silently spells out the letters. If, for example, he taps six times and the word you glimpsed has six letters, you can proceed.

Suppose you fail in any of the book tests described in this chapter? Mentalists have a marvelous out. Everyone knows that even the best subjects for parapsychology experiments are seldom 100 percent accurate. A failure convinces people that you are relying on mental agility, not trickery. Several years ago a professional mentalist missed not once but many times during guest appearances on television. Many of those who saw him were as impressed by his misses as his hits. One spectator told me, "He must be a legitimate telepathist; otherwise he would always succeed."

I would advise the reader to present mental feats he knows will work successfully as concluding numbers. Gamble if you must with earlier tests, but not with the one you do just before leaving the stage.

Conjuring with Cards

Someone using his or her own pack of cards can shuffle the pack, remove a card, then stare at it as he or she holds the card with its back turned toward you, and you can immediately name the card—under the right conditions. The conditions are these: there must be a light over the other person's shoulder; the card must be held in front of the person's face; and the person must be wearing glasses. While seeming to look straight into the person's eyes, you will be able to see the reflection of the card.

This trick is practical in the sense that it works, but it is useful only on very rare occasions.

The card magic in this chapter is of another sort. You can perform it for small groups or on a stage whenever you choose to. Neither complicated apparatus nor unusual digital skill is essential.

But remember: Avoid embarrassment by always asking those who select cards to remember them. I recall the expression on a noted performer's face when he asked a woman to name the card she had taken from the pack only a moment or so before, and she said, "I didn't look at it. You told me to remove a card and replace it."

131

When volunteers from the audience participate, card magic is as effective on a stage as it is when shown in more intimate surroundings.

SCARNE'S CONTROLLED CHOICE

Long before John Scarne became the nation's number-one authority on gambling, he earned his living as a professional magician. His skill with cards is extraordinary, and his presentations are psychologically sound.

This routine is an excellent example of his strategy. I have simplified the basic moves to make it more practical for those who do not have Scarne's dexterity.

The magician holds a borrowed, thoroughly shuffled pack of cards, face-down in his left hand. He shuts his eyes and begins dealing the cards face-up in a heap on the table. After six cards have been dealt, he says, "As I go through the cards, think of one the moment you see it pass." Three cards later, he asks, "Got it?" without slackening his pace. If the reply is affirmative, he knows a choice was made of the seventh, eighth, or ninth card, but continues to deal at least two more cards. If the answer is no, when he deals the twelfth card, he asks, "Got it now?" If the reply is yes, he knows that the tenth, eleventh, or twelfth card was selected.

Suppose the yes comes at this point. The magician deals a few more cards, then picks up the pile on the table and puts it face-down on the pack in his hand.

"Picture the card in your mind," the magician says as he shuffles the pack. (Scarne executes at this point a cutting maneuver that despite its complexity keeps the pack in its original sequence, but I suggest that you shuffle ten cards one by one to the bottom.) Place the pack face-down on the table. The bottom card (the tenth one shuffled there) is one of the three the spectator may have selected. The other two possible choices are at the top of the pack.

Take the uppermost card and insert it partway into the middle of the pack. Using the card as a lifting device, remove the upper pile, square it up, and place it face-down on the palm of the spectator's left hand. In squaring the pile, glimpse the bottom card. You now know that one of the three possible cards is at the bottom of the pile in the spectator's left hand, and you know the name of the card. Another possible card is at the top of this pile, and the third is at the bottom of the heap remaining on the table.

Pick up the remaining heap and tell the spectator to extend his right hand, palm up. As you give these instructions, tilt the pile and glance at the bottom card before you place the cards on the spectator's right-hand palm. You now know the names and locations of two of the possible cards and the location but not the name of the third.

Tell the spectator to name his card. The moment he does so, produce it. If it is not one of the bottom cards, it must be the one on the top of the pile in his left hand, so turn this card face-up. If it is one of the bottom cards turn that entire pile face-up to disclose the card.

You must learn how to turn the cards face-up at the start of the trick without varying the speed of the deal as you ask the necessary questions. The questions must be perfectly timed to limit a possible choice to three cards.

The impact of this feat is stronger than those in which cards are removed and replaced, because the onlooker merely thinks of a card. An amusing aspect is that you do not know the name of the selected card until it is spoken, but your quick disclosure of it makes it appear you were aware of the card's identity from the moment it was chosen.

Of course, if the spectator says he has "got it" after the ninth card is dealt, then the magician shuffles seven cards to the bottom of the deck; if the spectator says "yes" after the fifteenth card, the magician shuffles thirteen to the bottom of the deck, etc. The number that goes to the bottom of the pack is always two less than the highest number in whichever group of three the spectator chooses.

SEALED IN

One card, the king of diamonds, is sealed in an envelope. Another, the queen of clubs, is covered by the envelope. They change places instantly.

Carefully split in half a king of diamonds and a queen of clubs. Make a double-faced card by peeling off the backs and pasting the reverse sides of the two faces together. On occasion I have secretly added the double-faced card to a borrowed pack and performed with a borrowed envelope. You can imagine how astonishing the transposition was under those circumstances. When shown with your own cards, the effect is still amazing.

Take two cards from a face-up pack: an unprepared king of diamonds, and the queen of clubs with a king of diamonds on its reverse side. Put the cards face-up on a table, then display an unprepared envelope. Show that the envelope is empty. Say, "Remember these cards, the queen of clubs and the king of diamonds." Put the queen squarely on the king.

Show the back of the king as you slide the cards into the envelope. Close the flap, but do not seal it. While you talk, turn the envelope over. "Which cards are in the envelope?" A spectator names them. Reach in and remove the king. Drop it face-up on the table. This is the double card with the queen on the other side.

Seal the envelope. If there is a strong light nearby, hold the envelope to the light so the shadow of the card can be seen.

Place the envelope on the table. Put the king of diamonds on the envelope, then fold in the ends of the envelope to cover the card from view. Pick up the wrapped card with your fingers on the lower side of the envelope and with your thumb holding the folded sides together at the top. In moving the envelope to your left hand, turn your right hand palm down and take the reversed envelope between your left fingers and thumb.

"The queen is sealed inside; the king is outside. Now for an instant change." Tilt the envelope. The double card, with the queen facing up, slides out of the fold.

Immediately give the envelope to a spectator. "Note the envelope is still sealed, rip it open, and take out the card from inside." It is the king.

Neither this card nor the envelope has been prepared, so they may be examined thoroughly. You will find that the envelope is subjected to far more scrutiny than the card.

After you have given the sealed envelope to an onlooker, casually drop the face-up pack on the face-up queen and put the cards in your side pocket.

Have a queen of clubs ready there. If you do another card trick, bring this queen out with the pack and leave the double card in your pocket.

You can call the king Harry Houdini and the queen Bess Houdini and bill the card trick as a miniature version of their famous substitution trunk trick, Metamorphosis, in which Bess locked Harry into a trunk, then instantly switched places with him. This makes the performance more intriguing.

John Scarne, leading authority on gambling, was a master manipulator of playing cards long before he studied odds and percentages.

PING-PONG PLUS CARDS

Any deviation from the familiar attracts attention. Think back. What are the tricks you remember best from the last magic show you saw? Most likely, they are the ones that were new to you, or those that were presented with original touches.

Novelties fascinate. If an unusual presentation has a good plot, audience participation, and an applause-producing climax, it merits consideration for a place in your program.

With a stroke of his paddle, the magician bats a Ping-Pong ball out over the heads of the audience. The person who catches the ball is invited to bring it to the stage.

Once there, the spectator selects a card from a deck of face-down cards, marks the card by tearing away one corner, then returns it to the pack.

The magician shuffles the cards and places the pack on top of his Ping-Pong paddle. He is about to bat the cards when he decides that the feat will seem more difficult if the spectator also shuffle the cards.

Eventually, standing twelve feet away from the spectator, the magician tells him to toss the deck toward the paddle. The magician bats the cards, sending them up in the air. All fall to the floor but one. The selected card is seen face-up on the paddle. It is removed and given to the spectator. The corner torn away earlier is fitted to the card to prove this is the same one that was originally chosen.

The properties needed for this presentation are a Ping-Pong ball, a paddle, a pack of cards, and a dab of soft wax. If you cannot find adhesive wax, a small piece of transparent tape—the kind with sticky material on both sides—will do.

Ping-Pong paddles are available with various surfaces. Some have sandpaper; others rubber, plastic, or wood. I prefer those made of wood or plastic.

Fasten the adhesive to one side of the paddle. Most paddles are marked with the maker's name or insignia on one side of the handle. If the adhesive is put on this side of the paddle, you can be sure the prepared surface is uppermost by glancing at the handle.

The Ping-Pong ball is batted out with the unprepared side of the paddle. Don't drive the ball straight toward a spectator. Strike it so that it will arc high in the air, then fall.

The spectator who catches the ball is told to hold it above his or her head. Then, using the technique described in the first chapter of this book (see p. 3) the spectator is maneuvered out into the aisle and onto the stage.

The spectator is given a free choice of cards. He or she is instructed to tear away an index corner of the selected card, then to replace it in the pack. By riffling through the corners of the pack with his thumb, the magician can quickly locate the selected card. There is a slight click as the card with the missing corner is reached. Cut the deck to bring the selected card to the top. Then reverse the pack so this card is face-up at the bottom. Put the face-up pack on the sticky side of the paddle, firmly pressing the back of the chosen card so that it will adhere.

As you announce that you will let the spectator shuffle the cards thoroughly, turn the paddle so that the pack falls into your free hand and the selected card goes to the under side of the paddle.

After the spectator completes the shuffle, stand twelve feet away. Tell him or her to hurl the pack at the paddle. Bat the cards. They will soar up, then scatter. Turn the handle as they fall and bat again. Cards will fly in all directions—except the selected one, which appears on the paddle.

It will enhance the climax if you ask the spectator to name the selected card a moment before the pack is tossed toward the paddle. Then everyone will recognize it when they see it on the blade.

Handle the paddle with care after the chosen card has been affixed to it. Keep that side of the paddle turned away from the spectator and the audience. No one should suspect that the card is on the paddle when you give the spectator the pack to shuffle.

After the card is seen on the paddle, remove it, and tell the spectator to fit the piece earlier torn away. It is the missing corner.

If a Ping-Pong paddle isn't available, you can use a cloth-bound book instead, turning the book so the lower side, to which the selected card has been attached, is brought into view as you bat out the falling cards.

This should be the final number of a routine. It is a spectacular finish. For the middle-aged magician, there is an additional benefit: Each rehearsal will help to reduce your waistline as you bend to pick up the scattered cards from the floor.

Albert Goshman, an expert at sleight of hand, uses taped symphonic music to enhance his carefully planned presentations of close-up conjuring.

CHANCE OR COINCIDENCE

Hanging on the rear drape when the curtains open are eight large playing cards. The backs of the jumbo cards are to the front. They are in a row, ten inches apart.

Showing the faces of eight smaller cards—the size used for bridge—the magician calls out their names: "The six of clubs, the deuce of spades, the queen of hearts, the three of diamonds, the eight of diamonds, the jack of clubs, the three of hearts, and the ten of spades. These," he says, "are duplicates of the larger cards."

Turning the small cards face-down, he shuffles them, then invites a member of the audience to the stage to assist him. "The odds are against success in this experiment," the magician states as he puts the cards in the volunteer's right-hand coat pocket.

"Please hold your right hand in the air. Try to follow my instructions as rapidly as possible. Close your fingers. Open them. Close them. Open them. Reach into your pocket and pull out a card."

The magician takes the card. "By chance, the deuce of spades has been chosen." He displays it, then takes the volunteer to the side of the stage.

The magician points to the row of jumbo cards. "The large cards match the other cards. Call out any number from one to eight."

Suppose the spectator says five. The magician counts to the fifth card. Before he shows its face, he turns the fourth and sixth cards over so that their faces can be seen.

"Had you said four, you would have selected the three of diamonds. Had you said six, you would have chosen the queen of hearts. But you said five." The magician turns the face of the fifth card to the front. It is the duplicate of the card the spectator took from his pocket earlier—the deuce of spades.

Thanking the volunteer for his assistance, the magician says, "Chance . . . coincidence . . . or—?" He smiles, shrugs, then leaves the stage.

This concept won the first prize for professional originality at a national magicians' convention. Since then, I have found that it appeals as much to the public as to those who follow the most deceptive profession.

When the small cards are shuffled, the deuce of spades,

which was face-up on the bottom is shuffled to the top of the face-down pile. The cards are placed in the volunteer's pocket with their faces turned toward his body, and with the deuce on the outer side of the pile.

The finger closing-and-opening exercise prepares the volunteer to respond to your instructions rapidly. When he is told to reach into his pocket and remove one card, he takes the outside card—the deuce of spades—the first card his fingers touch. The magician asks the spectator to show the card to the audience and announce its name.

Paper clips are at the tops of the jumbo cards. Safety pins put through the upper loops of these clips fasten the cards to the rear drape.

The big cards have been placed with their backs to the front. The first, third, fifth, and seventh cards from the left are deuces of spades. The second, fourth, sixth, and eighth cards are the six of clubs, the three of diamonds, the queen of hearts, and the jack of clubs. The magician counts from right to left if an even number is called by the volunteer. The count is made from left to right when an odd number is chosen.

The magician and the volunteer are standing at the side of the stage facing the audience, with the cards to their right when the number is called. It will seem natural for the magician to begin his count with the closest card when an even number is selected, and just as reasonable for him to walk across the stage and begin the count at the left when an odd number is mentioned. Thus he can always end the count on a deuce of spades.

The showing of the cards adjacent to the deuce serves two purposes. It builds up the climax, and it suggests that all the large cards are different.

The trick may be done with six, ten, or twelve cards, but eight is the number I prefer. When no rear drape is available, I have thumbtacked the large cards to the wall.

What if the spectator does not pull the deuce of spades from his pocket? What would happen if, say, he withdrew the queen of hearts? I always carry an extra two of spades hidden in the breast pocket of my jacket. So far, I have not had to use it, but here's what I'd do in such a contingency:

I would take the queen, its back turned to the front, and put it in my breast pocket so that a portion of the card extended. Actually, the queen would be inserted behind the deuce and the deuce would be pulled up. As the backs of the cards are identical, this switch would not be suspected. It would be done as I explained to the volunteer how he should keep a portion of the card in sight when the card was in his breast pocket. Then I would put the deuce there.

Later, after he had selected a number and I had shown the large deuce of spades at this number, I would say, "The large card exerts a strange influence on the smaller one. Please take the card from your pocket and show it to the audience." The smaller card, of course, would now be a deuce of spades, too.

I may never have to use this alternate ending, but should the moment come when it is needed, I am prepared.

Before the magician puts the eight cards in the spectator's side pocket, he should ask the volunteer to transfer whatever is in that pocket elsewhere.

This feat was designed for a stage, but it also can be shown in a living room. It is especially effective when the large cards are pinned onto curtains drawn across a picture window.

Don't forget to ask the spectator for the seven cards still in his side pocket before he leaves your side.

Mentalists may wish to use ESP symbol cards instead of playing cards. If so, have an artist draw the following symbols on cardboard: square, circle, triangle, plus sign, star, crescent, wavy lines, and question mark.

The cards I displayed at a sales meeting of a large corporation had the names of that company's product on one and those of competitors on the others. The volunteer's seemingly free choices were cards with the names of the sponsoring firm's brand.

RIFFLE GLIMPSE

The twenty-six red cards are at the top of a deck of cards; the twenty-six black cards are beneath them. The magician spreads the face-down cards between his hands, pushing the cards to the right with his left thumb. After a volunteer has selected a card from the upper portion, the thumb continues moving the cards to the right. Thus when the chosen card is replaced, it is the only red card among the blacks in the lower portion.

Holding the cards so spectators cannot see the card faces, you can quickly learn the name of the selected one.

Jean Hugard, an expert magician and the author of several outstanding books on conjuring techniques, noted in one of his

The pet rat of Irish deceptionist June Merlin concentrates on Christopher's card shortly before The Festival of Magic *telecast on NBC-TV.*

unpublished manuscripts, which is now in my collection, a more subtle way to gain this information.

"Riffle off the cards with the ball of the right thumb preparatory to a [dovetail] shuffle. Sight the red card. It stands out among the blacks."

To do this, cut off the upper, or red, portion of the pack, then place it to your left on a table. The left thumb bends up the lower right-hand corners of these cards. The right thumb bends up the lower left-hand corners of the black pile. As you riffle, shuffle, or interlace the cards, keep your eyes on the indexes that fly past the ball of your right thumb. With practice, the single red card among the blacks can easily be spotted.

After the shuffle is completed, the red and black cards will be thoroughly mixed. There will be no evidence that the pack has been prearranged.

If you wish to bring the selected card to the top, hold the pack in your left hand before the shuffle. Riffle the lower left-hand corners with your right thumb. The moment the red card flicks by, lift the pile above the card with your left hand and place it at your left. Put the bottom pile, with the selected card on the top, at your right. Interlace the cards, so that the top card of the right-hand pile becomes the top card of the pack.

You will find that the first few times the cards fly past the ball of your thumb they will not fall singly. After you have experimented with the angle of the bend and the pressure of the thumb, you will learn how to control the cards effectively.

As you know just about where the red card was placed among the blacks, you will learn how to spot it quickly with a single glance.

CRIMP CUT

Another way to bring a chosen card to the top may be used with a shuffled borrowed pack. As before, spread the cards face-down between your hands for the selection to be made. After the card has been chosen, bend the lower right-hand corner of the card above it with the tip of the little finger of your right hand. This action is hidden by the spread of the cards.

Then lift the upper portion of the cards for the selected card to be replaced in its former position. The card with the bent corner will then be above it. Square up the cards and cut to the bent corner. Put the portion you cut away—with the bent card at the bottom—under the pack. The chosen card will now be face-down at the top.

THE SPINNER

This is a novel way to produce a selected card after it has been returned to the pack and the pack has been enclosed in its case. The case is tossed up, spinning in the air, then caught. As it is whirled up a second time, the chosen card appears at the performer's fingertips.

Insert the pack into its case with the chosen card at the top face-down. The tip of the left index finger secretly pulls the top card away from the others as the flap is being closed. The flap then goes between the rest of the pack and this card. The illustration shows how this is done.

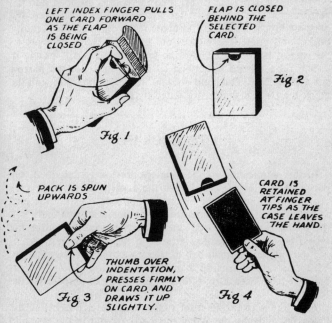

LEFT INDEX FINGER PULLS ONE CARD FORWARD AS THE FLAP IS BEING CLOSED

FLAP IS CLOSED BEHIND THE SELECTED CARD.

Fig. 1

Fig. 2

PACK IS SPUN UPWARDS

CARD IS RETAINED AT FINGER TIPS AS THE CASE LEAVES THE HAND.

THUMB OVER INDENTATION, PRESSES FIRMLY ON CARD, AND DRAWS IT UP SLIGHTLY.

Fig. 3

Fig. 4

Hold the case at the top between your right thumb and fingers. The thumb covers the portion of the chosen card that would otherwise be visible in the half-circle indentation at the top of the front of the case.

When you are ready to produce the card, press on it with your thumb, and pull it up just enough so that you can grip it between the ball of your thumb and the tip of your index finger as you spin the case in the air.

All eyes will follow the case as it turns. Members of the audience will be surprised when they look down and see the selected card in your hand.

Catch the case as it falls with your free hand.

PACK PENETRATION

In this variation, a rubber band is placed around the cardboard case holding the cards; then the case is dropped into the performer's side pocket. After the performer has asked the person who chose the card to name it, he dips his hand into his pocket and immediately takes out the card. When he removes the case, it is still closed, and the rubber band is still around it.

The rubber band is applied so that it encircles the narrow sides of the case. The band does not therefore interfere with the quick removal of the card isolated by the flap.

THE STICK-UP

In this application of the strategy previously described, the person who selected a card hurls the deck enclosed in the case at a magazine held by the magician. Those who expect the card to appear on the magazine are disappointed. "Apparently you threw the cards too hard," the performer says. He turns the magazine over. The card is sticking to the rear cover.

You will need a small ball of sticky wax for this presentation. You can carry it inside a matchbook, from which several matches have been torn, until you are ready to prepare for the feat.

Affix the wax to the front of the card case, just below the half-circle indentation. When the cards are put in the case and the chosen one is isolated by the flap, roll the ball of wax upward with your right-hand thumb and press it against the card.

Pick up the magazine with your left hand. Hold the card case, indentation side down, with your thumb as you show both the back and the front of the periodical. Put the case on the magazine. Press firmly with your thumb so that the card will adhere to the magazine, then turn it so that the case is away from the audience. Lift your thumb. The case will fall into your waiting right hand.

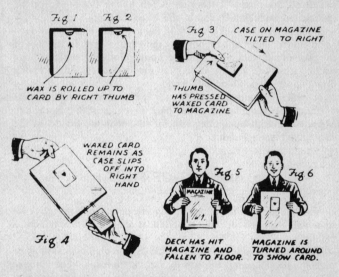

Fig 1   Fig 2

WAX IS ROLLED UP TO CARD BY RIGHT THUMB

Fig 3   CASE ON MAGAZINE TILTED TO RIGHT

THUMB HAS PRESSED WAXED CARD TO MAGAZINE

WAXED CARD REMAINS AS CASE SLIPS OFF INTO RIGHT HAND

Fig 4

Fig 5   DECK HAS HIT MAGAZINE AND FALLEN TO FLOOR.

Fig 6   MAGAZINE IS TURNED AROUND TO SHOW CARD.

Give the case to the spectator and stand several feet away, holding the magazine with your fingers in front and your thumbs at the back. When you tell the spectator to toss the case at the magazine, continue to keep card in place with your thumb. Otherwise the sudden impact might cause the card to dislodge.

When the card does not appear on the cover of the magazine, and just when it seems that the trick has failed, smile; then display the back of the magazine. Seemingly the card has penetrated the pages.

If you wish, you may use a book, a board, or a folded newspaper as a target instead of a magazine.

SHOOTING A CARD TO A WALL

In one of my night-club routines, I presented a modern version of a feat featured by Pinetti, the outstanding European conjurer of the eighteenth century.

An assistant held a wooden board, fourteen inches wide, sixteen inches long, and one inch thick. After the chosen card had been returned to the pack and brought to the top, I held the pack in my right hand and took a pistol, loaded with blanks, from my left-hand trouser pocket. I threw the pack at the board and fired the pistol. All the cards fell to the floor—except the chosen one, which adhered to the board.

A small ball of sticky wax had been on the nail of my left-hand index finger until I brought the chosen card to the top of the face-down pack. As I squared up the cards, I transferred the sticky substance to the center of the selected card, pressing down so the wax would adhere.

To practice the throw, put the cards face-down on the fingers of the right hand, holding the pack in place with the thumb. Move the thumb aside and push forward with the fingers as the cards leave your hand.

SLEIGHT OF FOOT

An unexpected finish adds to any presentation, especially one in which it seems—for the moment at least—that the trick has failed.

"You may have seen sleight of hand," the magician says as he puts his foot squarely on top of a pack of cards, "but I doubt that you have ever before seen sleight of foot." He explains that the pressure of his shoe will bring two previously chosen cards to the top of the pack. He lifts his foot, bends down, and flips over the two top cards. Alas, they are not the ones that had been selected. He shrugs, scoops up the cards, and drops the pack into his side pocket. Then he has an inspiration. "Perhaps I pressed too firmly." He sits down, takes off his shoe, and asks the closest onlooker to peer inside it.

Two cards are there, the onlooker reports. The magician removes them. They are the chosen cards.

A forcing pack is used in this feat. It has twelve sixes of diamonds at the top, as many fours of clubs beneath them, and twenty-eight randomly assembled cards at the bottom. With an arrangement of this sort, while holding the cards face-up, you can casually spread the lower portion to make it appear that all the cards are different.

With the pack held face-down and the top twelve cards fanned out, you can also ask an onlooker to touch, then take a card, and be certain that this card will be a six of diamonds. The performer, please note, does not ask the spectator to choose or select a card; he specifies touch. The cards are offered so only one of the twelve can be touched. With the second twelve cards offered in the same way, it is inevitable that a four of clubs will be tapped.

It is important that these cards be touched because you have a matching pair concealed in your shoe. The magician cuts the pack before the spectators are told to insert their cards near the center. The cut brings randomly assorted cards to the top.

Feign a look of disgust as you turn the two cards face-up then drop these cards and the rest of the pack into your side pocket. Without saying so, make it clear before you take off your shoe that your hands are empty.

The reason you have the onlooker peek in the shoe is to establish that the cards are already there before you reach in and extract them.

The pack is placed in your side pocket for two reasons. You would be embarrassed if you left the pack where a curious spectator could spread the cards face-up; by placing the pack there, you can subtly switch it for the one from which the cards in your shoe were removed before the performance.

By the outer side of the pack already in your pocket is a divider—an oblong piece of cardboard that is longer than the playing cards. Drop the cards you picked up from the floor so they will fall to one side of the divider. Later remove the cards from the other side. Without the cardboard, the two packs might become mixed together.

CARD ON WINDOWPANE

At lunch one afternoon many years ago, John Scarne told me how, after a little advance preparation before he rang the door-bell and was admitted to the house, he had amazed the dinner guests in a suburban home. For his final feat, he threw a pack

Milbourne Christopher made his Broadway debut with a one-man magic show at the Longacre Theatre in 1954. French star Jeanmaire was delighted by a backstage rising-card experiment. Her card popped up from the pack.

of cards across the room. It struck a closed window shade. The force of the blow triggered the spring in the roller. The shade shot up with a clatter, revealing the card a guest had chosen earlier fastened to the window behind the shade.

When the man who had selected the card went to remove it from the glass, he frowned. The card was on the *outer* side of the windowpane. Though he unlocked the window and opened it, he couldn't reach high enough to get the card.

Arranging for the card to appear on the far side of the window was a stroke a genius.

THE SENSITIVE FINGER

The magician tells a spectator to lift off about two thirds of the pack as it rests on a table. This second pile is put to the right of the other cards. The spectator is next instructed to lift about a third of the second pile and place it to the right of the second pile.

"Now shuffle one of the outer piles and replace it where it was. Then do the same with the other outer pile."

After this has been done, the magician says, "I think you will agree that neither you nor I know the positions of any of the cards in the piles you have shuffled. Please choose one."

Suppose the pile to the extreme right is selected. The magician asks the spectator to look at the top card, then return it. "Put the pile at the extreme left on the card, gather up the two piles, and place them on top of the one in the center. Finally, cut the pack and complete the cut."

Reaching for the cards, the magician ribbon-spreads the pack face-up so the indexes of all the cards are visible.

Telling the spectator to close his or her eyes and think of the card, the magician takes the index finger of the spectator's right hand between his right thumb and fingers, then moves the spectator's finger, held an inch or so above the cards, from one extremity to the other. Suddenly he touches the tip of the spectator's finger to a card and asks the spectator to open his or her eyes.

The spectator's finger is resting on the chosen card.

This astonishing revelation is possible because the magician knows the position of a *single* card in the pack he took from his pocket. The twenty-fifth card from the top is, say, the king of hearts. Because of the way the pack is distributed into piles, the king will be in the one that was not shuffled—the center pile.

The card at the top of the right-hand pile after the shuffle will be the twenty-fourth card above the king after the pack has been reassembled. The cutting of the pack does not alter the sequence of the cards.

When the pack is spread face-up, the chosen and thought-of card will be the twenty-fourth card to the *left* of the king. If, say, the king is the third card from the left end, count silently, beginning with the adjacent card, one, two; then count in from the right end, four, five, and so on, until you see the twenty-fourth card. This is the one you have the spectator's finger touch.

Now suppose the spectator had chosen the left pile instead of the right. He or she would have been instructed to look at and remember the *bottom* card, then put the left pile above the one at the extreme right and the center pile above the now larger right pile. In this case the selected card will be the *twenty-seventh* to the *right* of the king after the face-up spread is made.

A performer more interested in the mechanics of magic would simply point his own finger at the selected card. Those who hope to delight will ask the spectator to concentrate as he moves his or her finger and seemingly locates the card with the onlooker's sensitive digit.

CARD AND BALLOON

A selected card flies invisibly to the center of an inflated balloon. The cards may be borrowed; the balloon is unprepared. The feat may be exhibited in a living room or on a stage.

The chosen card is brought to the top of the pack with the Crimp Cut, explained earlier in this chapter: or if you use your own cards, have in your pack twelve sixes of diamonds, as in the Sleight of Foot trick. When one of them has been selected and replaced in the center, another remains as the upper card.

Give a balloon to a spectator, ask him or her to inflate it, then tie a knot so that the air cannot escape. Hold the pack face-down in your left hand with your right hand, fingers together, above it. Watch the balloon being blown up as you put the ball of your right index finger on the upper left corner of the top card. Slide the card half an inch forward, then press down with your finger. This action brings the top card pivoting up into your right hand. Your fingers conceal it from view. Retain the card by partially closing your fingers, then pick up the pack between thumb and index finger. This is a natural way to grasp it.

Ask for the inflated balloon. Transfer the pack to your left hand. Take the knotted end of the balloon between the right thumb and index finger.

Extending your left arm to the side, so the pack will be at least two feet from the balloon, request a spectator to touch the end of a lighted cigarette to the balloon. As the spectator approaches, clip the upper corner of the palmed card between your index and middle fingers. The moment the balloon explodes, the right fingers straighten, and the thumb goes behind the card to push it up so it can be gripped between the tips of the thumb and index finger. It will take practice to synchronize the sudden appearance of the card with the breaking of the balloon. When the flip-up move is mastered, it will create the illusion that the card was in the balloon.

If you perform with an unprepared pack, have the person who chooses the card write his or her initials on it in large letters with a felt-tip pen. Give the card away as a souvenir at the end of the feat.

Use round balloons, not those shaped like sausages. A red balloon is more interesting to most people than one of another color. If you wear a red jacket, a yellow balloon will stand out in contrast. If you wish, have the inflated balloon broken by a pin.

A drum roll as the spectator is about to break the balloon builds tension in a theatre. In a living room, riffle the corners of the pack with your left thumb to provide a rasping sound.

Ask the person who selected the card to call out its name before the balloon breaks. Then everyone present will see that the card you produce is the correct one.

Even though you do this, turn the face of the card to the selector when it appears and ask, "Right?" The yes that follows should produce immediate applause.

Cheap balloons are better for this feat than expensive ones. As the rubber is thinner, they break more readily.

INFALLIBLE PREDICTION

While having lunch or dinner with a friend, the magician announces he has made a prediction. He takes an envelope from his pocket, then slides it under an ashtray. He puts two cards face-up on the table—the two of hearts and the deuce of clubs.

"I've always been interested in how people respond. By studying them, I can tell how they will react to a specific problem. I thought of you this morning and visualized you choosing one of these cards. Then I wrote a prediction. Let's see how well I know you.

"You have a free choice. Try, if you wish, to outwit me. It would appear that you have a fifty-fifty chance of succeeding. Yet I am sure of the card you will choose, even though you have not as yet made a definite decision.

"Look at the cards. Take as long as you feel necessary to make a choice, then touch one."

The friend taps a card. The magician shows his prediction. The prediction is correct.

Don't bypass this feat because of its simplicity. Though the trick is easy to do, a good showman can make it tremendously effective.

The magician has written two predicitions: one on the underside of the envelope, the other on a piece of paper inside the envelope. No matter which card is chosen, one of these predicitions will prove to be right.

If the one inside the envelope matches the selection, the magician slides the envelope out from under the ashtray, tears it open, and pulls out the paper. If the one on the underside is required, he turns the envelope lower side up. In either case, he reads the words aloud as well as shows them. The paper may be presented to the other person as a memento. The prediction on the envelope, however, is returned to the performer's pocket after it has been displayed.

Use opaque envelopes and print, rather than write, the names of the cards. You can have a duplicate torn envelope in your inside breast pocket with the prediction on one side. In this instance, start to put the first envelope away, switch it for the duplicate, then say, "Maybe you'd like to have this for a souvenir."

This infallible method of making a prediction can also be

used with great effect to apparently forecast the outcome of a boxing match, football game, or tennis match.

Thumbtack the envelope to a door before you watch the event on television, or listen to it being described on the radio. If you use this procedure during a stage performance, call attention to the envelope fastened to a piece of scenery or a curtain or wall at the start of your show.

It is the presentation not the method that makes magic memorable.

Johnny Carson began his show-business career as a magician. Milbourne Christopher has made many appearances with him on his NBC-TV program.

Rope Mysteries

The first feat of magic I saw as a boy was the cut and restored string. My father, who was not a professional magician, amazed me with this when I was six. He taught me how to do it, and I performed it for visitors to our house in Baltimore. Later as a scout, I became so fascinated with knots that I read sailors' manuals and studied anthropological treatises that described the string games of "primitive" tribes.

In my teens, I devised a way to create the illusion that I could stretch a rope. This trick won a prize at a regional convention of the International Brotherhood of Magicians in Lancaster, Pennsylvania.

There were many specialists when I played my first engagements in nightclubs and theatres. Gus Fowler, for example, conjured with watches and clocks, and Ade Duval worked his wonders with silk foulards. I became a specialist in rope magic. At the age of twenty-one, I sailed for my first tour of Europe with Fred Sanborn, a noted pantomimic comedian. My picture then appeared on the cover of *The Sphinx*, the leading periodical in the conjuring field at the time and John Mulholland, editor of *The Sphinx*, said I was to be congratulated for "getting off the beaten track" with my act. It was a fortunate way to begin a career.

In this chapter I have gathered together several of my favorite tricks with rope. Some are designed for close-up presentation; others are more suitable for a stage.

SLIPPERY SQUARE KNOT

The most provocative close-up feats with rope are those that appear to be easy to do—until somebody tries them. This unusual knot trick ranks high in that category. The magician ties a square knot, then makes it dissolve.

Spectators who learned how to tie standard knots during their scouting or seafaring days are fascinated by this demonstration. Square knots, they know, can be subjected to great strain without slipping. Yet the magician causes one to fall apart. Those who insist on taking the rope and trying to do this themselves will be disappointed. Some will give up after a few attempts; others will spend hours without discovering the secret. This is because they are not familiar with the thief knot—a knot that seems to be a square knot but isn't.

According to legend, cautious deckhands aboard early sailing ships used this knot to fasten their sea bags. Then they could tell at a glance if someone had opened a bag and pried through their possessions while they were on duty.

Both ends of a rope are at the top in a square knot. Only one is there when a thief knot is formed. You can display a thief knot so it will appear to be a square knot if you push the lower end up and cover the point where it crosses the longer strand with your thumb.

Square and thief knots are shown side by side in the first two illustrations. The third and fourth indicate how the short end is moved and held so that a thief knot will be mistaken for a square knot.

The fifth and sixth drawings depict how a rope is held when you tie a thief knot. Put end A over end B. Press the two together between your right-hand thumb and index finger. Reach behind B, clip A near the tip between the middle and ring fingers of your left hand. Bring A to the left behind B, forming a loop. Still gripping A, extend your left index finger to bend B down behind the loop. Then, with your left thumb, push the end through the loop. Refer to the first illustration to see if the knot has been correctly made.

With the fingers of both hands closed around the rope at the sides of the knot, shove the short end at the right up; then position it as shown in the fourth illustration.

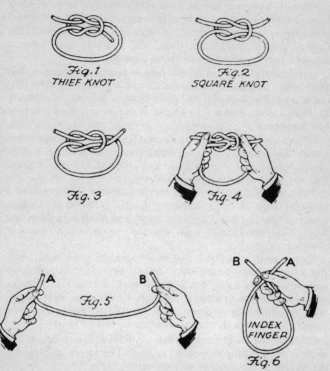

Fig. 1
THIEF KNOT

Fig. 2
SQUARE KNOT

Fig. 3

Fig. 4

Fig. 5

A   B

Fig. 6

B   A

INDEX
FINGER

With practice, you can tie a thief knot in three seconds. To make the knot dissolve, move your hands apart, letting the ends slip free from your thumbs and index fingers.

It will add to the presentation if you turn your left hand toward your body and your right hand away as the knot evaporates. It is not necessary to tug the rope, the knot unties automatically.

Until my old friend, Dean Longfellow, tied a thief knot for me many years ago in Washington, D.C., I had never seen one. Since then, I have presented this dissolving trick not only for intimate groups, but also on many stages.

CAMEL OR DROMEDARY?

"Camels have two humps," the magician says, as he bends a loop of rope to form two loops. He extends the first two fingers of his right hand, puts a finger through each loop. He closes the fingers quickly, straightens them, and a single loop appears between the fingers. "Dromedaries have one!"

It is doubtful that this information will amaze audiences, but the sudden change of two loops to one almost invariably produces a request to repeat the rapid change. When spectators try to duplicate the move, they find it is not as easy to do as they had imagined.

Unlike the Slippery Square Knot, this close-up puzzler is not a trick. There is no concealed secret; you do not attempt to hide the movements of your fingers. Yet even the keenest observer will not remember precisely what you did.

To master the moves, follow the illustrations. The center of a piece of rope is taken between the right thumb and index finger, as the left hand folds the rope, and holds it to form two loops. The left thumb holds the rope as shown in the first drawing.

Extend and spread the first two fingers of your right hand. Put a finger through each loop. Quickly bend your fingers down and around the rope. Bring your fingers together to clip the rope, release it with your left thumb, then extend your fingers with the single loop between them. The third drawing shows the fingers just before they press together to form a single loop.

Practice the finger movements until you can produce the single loop instantly. Speed is essential. The knack of blending the actions is not difficult to acquire.

When I presented this stunt as a part of a rope routine, I peered through the two loops and said, "Spectacles"; then I raised the single loop to one eye with the word, "Monocle."

Children are amused when I identify the double loops as rabbit ears and call the single one a rabbit tail.

THE FINGER FLING

This is another swifter-than-the-mind maneuver. The eye sees what happens, but the mind is confused. It can be performed with rope, tape, or string. One moment a loop is around the magician's thumb; the next, another loop circles his index finger.

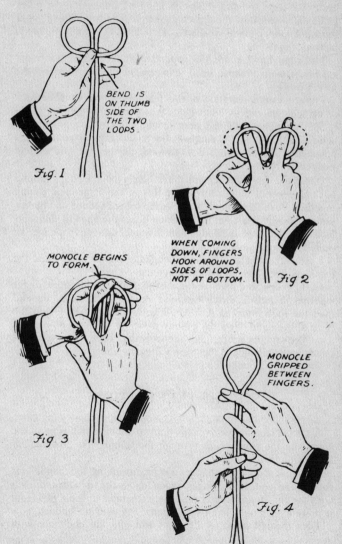

BEND IS ON THUMB SIDE OF THE TWO LOOPS.

Fig. 1

WHEN COMING DOWN, FINGERS HOOK AROUND SIDES OF LOOPS, NOT AT BOTTOM. *Fig 2*

MONOCLE BEGINS TO FORM.

Fig. 3

MONOCLE GRIPPED BETWEEN FINGERS.

Fig. 4

Three drawings illustrate the "before," "during," and "after" positions of the left-hand thumb and fingers. The left index finger pulls the left strand to the right, then immediately bends under the rope and straightens, flinging a loop around the index finger. If you follow the drawings with a rope looped over your thumb and persevere, you will learn how the index finger is bent and twisted.

The right hand keeps the rope taut as the left index finger manipulates it. Practice until you can get the loop around the finger quickly.

Preface a demonstration of this feat with words to this effect: "You will see exactly what I do. Watch closely; then try to do it." Sympathize with the person who tries to duplicate your actions. If he or she is successful at once, express your honest amazement. Dean Longfellow showed me this. He said he had learned it from a sailor.

I added a finish. After you have displayed the loops around both finger and thumb, press the tips of the finger and thumb together. Push the rope forward through the hole formed by this juncture with your right hand which holds the ends of the rope. You will find that the loops will dissolve, and the rope can be pulled out and away.

I also hit upon an alternate conclusion to be used when the rope has been tied in a loop previously.

In this variation, press the tips of the thumb and index finger together as before. Bring the long strands of the rope up and over the loop, marked A in the illustration, so they fall at the back of the hand. Now, by pulling down on the loop A, you can draw the strands up through the opening. Then, turn your left hand to the right, and the rope will fall clear.

THUMB PENETRATION

After looping a rope over his thumb, the magician tugs on the ends, and the rope passes through the thumb. The illustrations show how this is done.

The first drawing indicates the positions of the hands and rope. Bend your index finger, reach across the right strand, then with the tip of your finger pull the left strand to the right. Hold it there as the right hand puts opening A over the thumb.

Turn the left hand to the right and pull the ends taut with

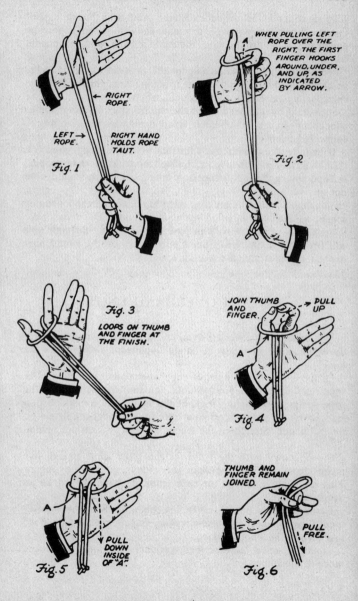

RIGHT ROPE.

LEFT ROPE.

RIGHT HAND HOLDS ROPE TAUT.

Fig. 1

WHEN PULLING LEFT ROPE OVER THE RIGHT, THE FIRST FINGER HOOKS AROUND, UNDER, AND UP, AS INDICATED BY ARROW.

Fig. 2

Fig. 3

LOOPS ON THUMB AND FINGER AT THE FINISH.

JOIN THUMB AND FINGER.

PULL UP

A

Fig. 4

A

PULL DOWN INSIDE OF "A".

Fig. 5

THUMB AND FINGER REMAIN JOINED.

PULL FREE.

Fig. 6

your right hand. Lift the index finger, press it to the tip of your thumb. Whenever you wish to create the illusion that the rope penetrates your thumb, give the ends a yank with your right hand.

Note that the right thumb keeps the two strands apart at the first stage of the trick. Otherwise, opening A might not be large enough to pass easily over your thumb. You will see that one loop is held by another behind the thumb after opening A goes over your thumb. As the left hand turns, this overlapping is concealed from view.

If you practice with the illustrations in front of you, you should have no difficulty mastering this trick. It may be performed with a piece of string or a length of ribbon should rope not be available.

Your eyes should be on your right hand, not on the left index finger, as the rope is lifted over your thumb. Once you have learned how to get the rope in position for the tug-through, you will find that if the right fingers pull harder on the strand now to your right, the release will be easier.

INSTANT OVERHAND KNOT

My method of tieing an overhand knot with one hand produces the knot instantly. A single downward swoop does the trick.

Drape a five-foot length of rope over your right hand. The rope rests adjacent to your thumb. The 16-inch short end of the rope hangs down at the back of the hand; the longer portion falls across the palm. Bend your little finger under the strand on the palm side. Straighten the finger, bringing the strand behind it.

Swoop down with the hand, catching the short strand, five inches from the end, between the index and middle fingers. This rapid move throws the rope from the hand and forms an overhand knot.

Earlier descriptions of this tie say that a quick upward movement flips the short end to the waiting fingers, then a downward toss throws the knot in place.

A single action, as described, produces the knot faster and more mysteriously.

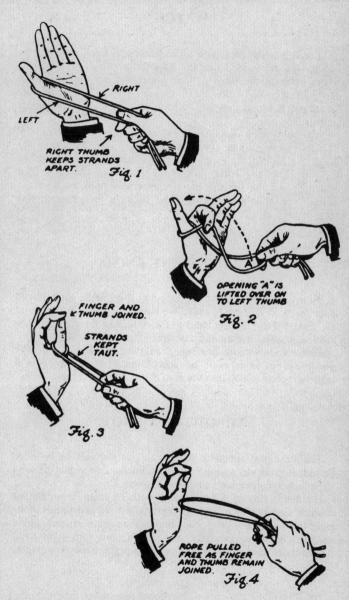

RIGHT

LEFT

RIGHT THUMB
KEEPS STRANDS
APART. *Fig. 1*

OPENING "A" IS
LIFTED OVER ON
TO LEFT THUMB
Fig. 2

FINGER AND
THUMB JOINED.

STRANDS
KEPT
TAUT.

Fig. 3

ROPE PULLED
FREE AS FINGER
AND THUMB REMAIN
JOINED. *Fig. 4*

WATCH!

Thread a wristwatch with a flexible metal band on the rope before you perform. Have the watch concealed in your right hand, bending the strap so that pressure from the tip of the second finger holds the watch to your palm. Tie the Instant Overhand Knot, as described above, and the watch will appear tied to the rope.

I first presented this during an appearance on the NBC-TV "Today" show. When I was introduced, I said, "It's time for magic." I flicked the rope. The watch materialized knotted to the rope. I looked at the face of the watch as I untied it, then added, "And the time is exactly seventeen minutes after the hour." The hour was not specified because the program was seen in several time zones.

TWO INSTANT KNOTS

With your hands twelve inches apart, display the rope draped over them so that an Instant Overhand Knot can be tied with each hand. Turn the left hand to the right, and the right hand to the left as the fingers swoop down to catch the ends.

This requires more practice than tying a single knot. The downward motions must be synchronized so the knots will come simultaneously into view.

THROWING A KNOT

The time you spend to master this throw will be well invested. It produces a knot instantly, and the throw may be used to tie a bracelet to the center of the rope.

Hold the tips of a five-foot length of rope between the thumbs and first two fingers of your outstretched hands, your right hand placed seven inches higher than your left one. Move your left hand horizontally to the right, and your right hand horizontally to the left. As the strand hanging from your right-

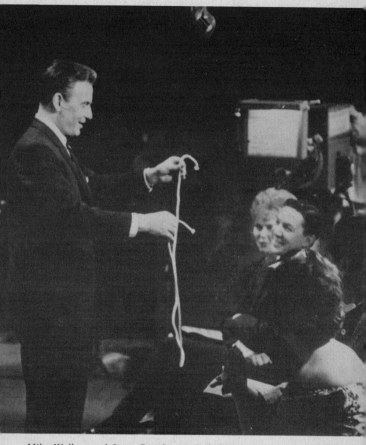

Mike Wallace and Joyce Davidson took front-row seats for Christopher's second hour-long performance on PM East.

hand fingers passes your left hand on the far side, a loop is formed. Throw the end in your right-hand fingers through this loop to produce a knot.

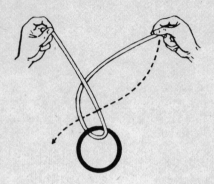

After you have learned how to toss the end of the rope accurately, you can make the trick more effective by keeping your hands apart, swinging the rope to form a loop, then throwing the right end through the loop. The illustration shows how this loop is made.

If a bracelet has been previously threaded on the rope, the knot will tie it in place. The second illustration shows the bracelet after it has been knotted.

A silk handkerchief that has been draped diagonally over the rope can also be tied to it with this throwing motion.

BRACELET FROM ROPE

The magician threads a bracelet on a rope, then invites a spectator to tie the bracelet with an overhand knot. The magician holds the bracelet in one hand, then pulls the rope away with the other hand. The bracelet comes free, though the knot is still tied.

As the illustration indicates, a knot can be opened wide enough for a bracelet to pass through it. Once the bracelet leaves the knot, the fingers of the right hand grip it, and the left hand tugs the rope. The bracelet slides off the rope when the left hand pulls.

You may present this trick extemporaneously with a borrowed finger ring and a piece of string. If, however, you use heavier cord, the feat is easier to perform.

As you make the knot larger and push the ring through it, divert attention from your actions by talking and shield your movements with your hands.

KNOTTED BRACELET RELEASE

After a borrowed bracelet has been threaded on a rope, several knots are tied above it. Though spectators to the left and the right of the magician hold the ends of the rope, he makes the knots disappear.

You must tie a loose square knot exactly like the one in the illustration. If it is made with the loops reversed the trick will not work. The right end of the rope is then brought through the lower opening, around the end, into the upper loop from the back, and out. Follow the dotted line in the drawing. Make this tie quickly, then ask two spectators to hold the ends of the rope.

As the bracelet hangs from the rope, a part of its upper surface will be visible as you glance down at the knot. Caution the spectators not to release the ends of the rope; take the upper surface of the bracelet between the index fingers and thumbs, open the loop, then push the bracelet through it. The knot will dissolve immediately, and the bracelet will be threaded on the rope as it was before the knot was tied.

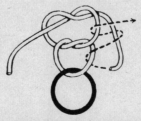

Christopher was in his teens when he invented Stretching a Rope. Since then, he has performed it in 70 countries and most of the American states.

I found that when a bracelet was tied to the rope with what is generally called a Chefalo knot, it could be released as described. This knot far predates the Italian illusionist Chefalo. Indeed, Chefalo told me when I met him in Berlin that Will Goldston, the prolific British author of conjuring books, had attributed the knot to him without Chefalo's knowledge.

At least a hundred years before Chefalo was born, superstitious British farmers would tie such a knot and release it believing that this action could cure sick cows. The knot is not recommended for this purpose, but it is one that every magician who performs rope tricks should know.

THROUGH THE WRIST

The magician places a loop of rope over his extended left wrist; then he again circles his wrist with the rope. He immediately pulls one of the strands forward, and the rope mysteriously penetrates his wrist.

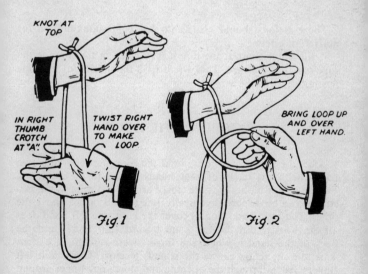

KNOT AT TOP

IN RIGHT THUMB CROTCH AT "A".

TWIST RIGHT HAND OVER TO MAKE LOOP

Fig. 1

BRING LOOP UP AND OVER LEFT HAND.

Fig. 2

The drawings illustrate each step of this procedure. Note that the knot is above the wrist. Note, too, the unusual way the right hand enters the loop to drape the rope over the wrist. Take one of the indicated strands between your right index finger and thumb, then pull to release the rope.

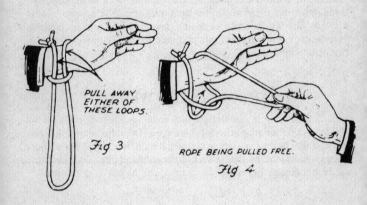

PULL AWAY
EITHER OF
THESE LOOPS.

Fig 3

ROPE BEING PULLED FREE.

Fig 4

These actions should blend into one continuous motion for maximum effect.

If the knot is not at the top, it may catch in the loop as the rope is pulled forward. This would spoil the illusion of the rope passing through the wrist.

LOOPING THE LOOP

After the rope comes free, hold the loop between your two hands, with the backs of your hands turned to the audience. The fingers of both hands are closed around the rope so the two strands can be displayed vertically, one several inches above the other. The right-hand fingers cover the knot; the left hand does all the work. Turn the left hand toward your body until the back of the hand is where the fingers were a moment earlier. This turning action causes the strands to cross. Open your left fingers, reach through the opening and close your finger around the upper strand of the opening to your right. Move your hand quickly to the left, sliding it along the rope as you do so. This forms a loose knot around the parallel strands, near the center.

To make the knot disappear, quickly release the rope in your left hand, close your fingers around the upper strand to the right of the knot, then slide your hand along the strand to the left.

The knot should be made rapidly. After it has been displayed, it should be dissolved with equal speed.

TOGETHER AGAIN

Though a cover is used in this cut-and-restored mystery, it enhances rather than detracts from the feat. The cover is a metal tube, three inches in diameter and eight inches long. It is not the simple tube it appears to be, as you will note in the illustration. Soldered inside it is a tapering tube. The wide end of this is soldered flush inside one end of the outer tube. The tapering end of the inner section provides a secret space in the tube.

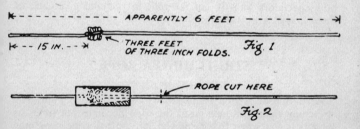

As the audience sees the trick, a six-foot length of rope is displayed, then threaded through the tube. A spectator cuts the rope in half. The cutoff piece is put into the tube. Spectators grasp the ends of the rope protruding from the tube. The magician, who holds the tube, tells the spectators to pull when he says, "Restore." They do so. The rope is once more six feet long; it is brought out of the tube in one piece.

To prepare for this trick, pleat three feet of a nine-foot length of rope in three-inch folds, fifteen inches from one end. The pleated portion is held secure by wrapping the rope around it, then tucking a loop under the outer strand (see illustration).

When the rope is displayed, the pleated section is concealed by your closed left hand, and the rope appears to be six feet long.

Thread the long end through the wide side of the tube, as pictured in the drawing. Pull the rope through the tube until the pleated section is hidden from view. About ten inches of the rope should remain hanging down on the side the rope entered. The larger portion extends to the right.

Holding the tube upright, with the left-hand palm on the top, and the right hand displaying the rope, ask a spectator to cut the rope at about the middle.

Tuck the cut portion into the tube in the space between the secret insert and the inner wall of the tube. Ask the person who did the cutting to hold the end of the rope protruding from the tube to the right, and invite another spectator to grasp the end extending from the tube to the left.

The palms of your hands placed over the ends of the tube will prevent anyone from seeing inside it.

As you say, "Restore," and the spectators pull on their ends of the rope, the pleated section unfolds. The rope is again six feet long.

Take the rope from the tube, then offer it as a souvenir. If both spectators want it, cut the rope in two and give each of them half to keep them happy.

STRETCHING A ROPE

A short rope is first stretched twice its original length. The stretching then continues until the rope becomes ten times as long as it was when first displayed. Any soft flexible rope may be used. The feat is essentially an optical illusion produced by manipulation.

To prepare for the performance, take off your coat. Hold the ends of a fifteen-foot length of rope, twelve inches from each end, in your left hand. Your right hand inserts the middle of the rope into your right hip pocket, then carefully folds the rope in the pocket so it will not snarl when it is withdrawn later.

Transfer the two ends of rope to your right hand, and put on your coat. As you do so, your right hand carries the two ends of rope down your right sleeve. Fold back one of the ends so that when your right hand closes, this end extending beyond your little finger is gripped by your ring and little fingers. The other end protrudes from the thumb side of your closed hand.

With the back of your right hand turned toward the front, it will appear that you are carrying in your hand a short piece of rope in a natural way. Walk to the center of the stage with your right side turned toward the audience. Extend your left hand, palm upward, slightly to the left in front of your body. Your right hand, with its back to the audience, places the strand that extends from the thumb side of your closed right hand across the palm of your left hand so that the rope hangs down on the thumb side. The closed right hand is kept adjacent to the left hand as the left-hand fingers close and grip the rope.

Keeping your left hand motionless, apparently pull with your right hand and stretch the rope. Actually the closed right hand slides along the rope as it comes from your sleeve, but the illusion is created that the rope is being pulled away from your left hand. Turn your body to the left as the lengthening is made. Loop the rope around your left hand, which opens to take it, after the first stretch. Stretch, then loop again, and continue to stretch until the entire rope has come into view.

Never pull with your left hand. This would destroy the illusion. Keep your eyes fixed on your motionless left hand as each lengthening occurs. You will not fully appreciate the stretching illusion until you go through the movements in front of a mirror.

When I first presented this feat, I entered with two ropes in my right hand. I took one and tossed it to a spectator. I asked him to examine it, then attempt to stretch it. He said it was unstretchable. Then I began stretching the rope I had retained.

The stretching feat is a strong opening for a rope routine. After the rope has been lengthened, it can be used for another trick.

MULTIPLYING ROPE

Bowing to acknowledge the applause he has received for the previous feat, the magician states that in addition to stretching rope, he can make rope multiply. He taps the coil in his left hand, then shows that he has changed it into two coils. The second rope is as long as the first.

The second coil has been tucked under the performer's belt

above his left hip pocket so that the loops are covered by his coat but within reach.

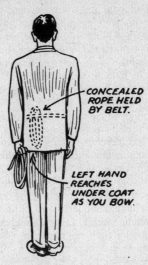

CONCEALED ROPE HELD BY BELT.

LEFT HAND REACHES UNDER COAT AS YOU BOW.

As he bows, his left hand, holding the coiled rope, reaches for the hidden coil of rope and adds it to the one in his hand. Spectators are not looking for a deceptive move when the steal is made. They are not aware that the second coil has been secured.

After he taps the rope, the magician separates the two coils. Taking an end of a coil in each hand, he raises his hands and allows both coils to unwind.

The second coil also can be added to the first with an alternate deceptive move. Holding the initial coil in his right hand, the magician reaches in his shirt pocket for a pencil. Draped over the pencil which is covered by his coat is the second coil. When the magician takes out the pencil, he also, without the audience's being aware of it, takes out the coil. The pencil is transferred to his left hand. It is used to tap the rope in his right hand; then the coils are separated and displayed.

SUPER STRETCH

Shortly after I had worked out a way to stretch a rope, I devised a method to stretch an *examined* rope. You will remember that in the original presentation, one rope was thrown to a spectator and a second was lengthened.

In this variation, two ropes also play a part. One is three feet long; the other measures twenty feet from end to end. A knot is tied in one end of the longer rope. This end is put in the right hip pocket, then the strand is pleat-folded above it. The far end is held in the right hand as the performer dons his coat.

He enters with the end hidden in the crotch between his thumb and index finger, carrying the shorter rope between his fingers. The short rope is displayed by his left hand, then tossed to an onlooker. After the rope has been examined, the spectator throws it back to the magician. He catches it with his left hand and holds one end between his thumb and index finger. The right hand closes around the dangling rope, then slides down it. The right hand brings the lower end to the left-hand fingers—or seems to, for it is, in fact, the end of long rope that the left fingers grasp. Turning his body to the left, the magician slides his right hand down the end four inches. His right fingers press the end of the short rope against the long rope extending from his sleeve. The left hand releases the end of the short rope it originally held.

At this point, the short rope seems to be in the performer's right hand. It is, but the end that protrudes from his fist is that of the longer rope.

The stretching process begins as in the earlier version. The left hand, palm up, closes on the rope placed there by the right hand. The right hand stretches the rope and continues to stretch it until the knotted end of the long rope reaches the right thumb and index finger. Then the left hand drops the coil it has been holding to the floor. The final sequence is presented very rapidly.

The left hand now goes to the right hand and closes around the rope. The right hand does not move. The left slides along the rope to the left. Seemingly the rope stretches again. Actually this length has been pulled up from the floor—through the left fingers. This time, after each stretch, the right hand holds the coil, and the process continues until all the rope is in the right hand.

This method is useful when the feat is presented as an encore. The end of the long rope that runs down the sleeve is held by a wide rubber band above the wrist, until the performer leaves the stage. In the wings, he quickly takes the end from the rubber band and grips it in the crotch between his thumb and index finger. Then he is ready to show the short rope—and stretch it.

STRETCHING A RIBBON

.For obvious reasons, I have never stretched a rope while wearing a bathing suit. I have, however, stretched strings and ribbons. A long cord or a ribbon can be tucked inside a 2-inch metal ball through a ¾-inch hole.

Concealing the ball in the closed fingers of his right hand, the magician displays a short ribbon in his left hand. The left hand brings the ribbon to the right hand and palms the ball as the right hand takes the ribbon. The ribbon is returned to the left hand, and the concealed ball is returned to the right hand.

The right hand slides down the ribbon as the left fingers hold it, then brings the lower end to the left hand. As in the rope method, the left-hand fingers take the end of the long strand from the ball, and the closed right-hand fingers press the end of the short ribbon to it. The strand extending from the ball is then stretched in the way already described.

At the end of the trick, the ribbon is gathered up, and it and the ball, hidden by the ribbon, are put aside.

The ball that holds the ribbon is changed from hand to hand during the trick so each hand, in turn, may be shown freely.

PRESENTING ROPE MAGIC

Resist the temptation to add color to rope magic by dyeing the strands various colors. Audiences will think that a red, green, or blue rope is so unusual that it must have been specially prepared, but they are familiar with ordinary white rope.

When rope tricks are shown against dark backgrounds and are adequately lighted, they can be presented effectively in large theatres.

If soft woven ropes are used, knots can be tied in massive strands as well as in less bulky lengths, as this photograph shows.

Any knot will not be visible at a distance if you wear a white or very light-colored jacket. If you have a choice of stage backgrounds, dark scarlet or deep purple drapes are excellent for contrast. Avoid, if you can, curtains with designs that will distract from your performances.

Amusing talk is as important as skillful manipulation. Without it, even the best tricks are far less entertaining.

Replace any rope that starts to turn gray with usage. The whiter the rope, the better it can be seen.

Contrary to what you may have read, the most famous rope trick has never been done the way it is described. Almost everyone has heard about the magician in India who threw a rope skyward, then caused it to remain suspended in space as his assistant climbed it and disappeared in the clouds above. Many illusionists, however, have presented variations of this onstage.

In vaudeville, I would enter with a long coiled rope, then tell about the marvelous feat. When I asked, "Is there a small Hindu boy in the audience?" and no one came forward, I would toss the rope into the wings and say, "No Hindu boy, no Indian rope trick."

One night in Providence, Rhode Island, a small Indian boy rushed from his seat in the third row to the stage. When I asked him if he had ever seen the fabulous mystery, he said, "No." I commented, "Neither have I," thanked him for his testimony, and went on with the show.

I had not said that I intended to perform the legendary feat, I had merely described it, so I was not embarrassed when this son of a New Delhi diplomat made his presence known. After that experience, however, I changed the wording of the introduction and said, "Is there in the audience a small Hindu boy named Pratal Ravi Chundra?" Possibly there may have been, but one never ran down the aisle.

One final tip: Wind the ends of the rope you use for knot tricks with strong white thread, then tie the thread securely. This keeps the ends from fraying.

Instruction to young volunteers should be clear and easy to follow. The magician's purpose is to amaze, not confuse, them.

Magic for Youngsters

Many magicians perform frequently for very young audiences at birthday parties and at school and church events. They change their programs when they play repeat engagements and are always searching for something new. With their needs in mind, I've designed several pieces of uncomplicated but showy equipment. The equipment can be built in home workshops by those who are handy with tools.

The stories that are told with these tricks will amuse the parents as much as their progeny. Not every child who would like to come on the stage to assist has the opportunity. All can participate in the show by shouting magic words.

RONALD RABBIT

"This is my new assistant, Ronald," the magician says as he turns toward the cutout figure of a standing rabbit on his table. "Ronald made his first appearance in a large folding top hat. One day I crushed the hat not knowing that Ronald was hiding in it. He has been this thin ever since. He was once a much fatter rabbit."

Two children are invited to take cards from an alphabet pack, then to return them after they memorize the letters they have chosen.

The magician inserts the pack in a holder between the painted rabbit's paws.

"When the audience counts to three," he says, addressing the rabbit, "push the chosen cards up from the pack immediately." The performer turns to the audience. "All together now, let's count. One . . . two . . . three!" There is no response from the rabbit. The cards do not appear.

"Perhaps we should count louder. Let's try again. One . . . two . . . three!" Despite the increased volume, the rabbit ignores the cue.

The magician shows his annoyance. "Ronald," he says, "the cards should pop up at three. Use your ears." The rabbit does. A selected card appears instantly on each tip.

As you can see by the illustration, this device is easy to make. Cut the rabbit from plywood, paint it, then attach the card holder and the two springs. The flat metal rods have clips at the ends, into which duplicates of the cards are fitted. The rods are folded back. The cards are held in place with a simple catch or a slide pin. The magician releases the catch or the pin when he tells the rabbit to use his ears. The springs propel the rods and bring the cards into view. A simple method to insure that the

The White House lawn, Easter Monday 1935. Milbourne Christopher performs for Mrs. Franklin D. Roosevelt, her friends and her grandchildren.

correct cards are selected is explained in the chapter on card tricks.

My friend, P. C. Sorcar, India's most famous magician, presented a giant-size version of Ronald in his elaborate illusion show. Sorcar added an extra touch. The moment the cards appeared, the rabbit's pink eyes lighted.

The response to Ronald Rabbit from magicians in many parts of the world was so enthusiastic that I introduced . . .

FORGETFUL FREDDY

A cutout figure of a small boy with a distraught expression stands on a table as the magician tells the story of Forgetful Freddy: "He could never remember where he put things. He misplaced his crayons, his picture books, and his scooter. One day his mother said that if he wasn't careful, he would lose his head. And he did."

The magician removes the head from the painted schoolboy and slips it into his pocket.

"Freddy looked most peculiar as he walked around without his head. He could not see where he was going. He bumped into chairs and fell down the stairs. The only advantages were that he didn't have to wash his face, comb his hair, or brush his teeth. He couldn't watch his favorite television show; he couldn't eat—not even lemon meringue pie. Finally, his mother blew up a balloon and tied it to his shoulders."

The magician pauses to do this, then continues, "She drew eyes, a nose, ears, and a mouth. When his friends saw him, they laughed and called him Balloon Head. No boy likes to be called Balloon Head, so he came to me for help. I'll show you how I solved his problem, if you will shout the magic word, 'Recess.' "

As this word fills the air, the balloon breaks, and Freddy's head reappears on his shoulders.

Children understand Freddy's problem. Adults do, too. The necessary equipment is small enough to pack flat in a slender case, yet large enough to be effective on stage.

The twenty-inch-tall Freddy fits upright into a slot in the

Between large-scale illusions, Christopher invited children to the stage in Magicworld, *at the Madison Square Garden Felt Forum in December 1968.*

HOLDER FOR BALLOON.

PEG → OF THE DETACHABLE HEAD FITS INTO HOLE ON SHOULDERS.

FRONT VIEW SHOWING THE SLOTTED BASE TO HOLD FIGURE.

BACK VIEW SHOWING SPRING AND METAL ARM.

NEEDLE

RELEASE CATCH

BALLOON TIED IN PLACE OF HEAD, IS PUNCTURED BY NEEDLE WHEN HEAD REAPPEARS.

detachable base. The head first seen has a wooden peg at the bottom. The second head has a sharp needle extending from the nose. The peg of the first head is inserted into a hole at the top of Freddy's shoulders. The illustration shows how the second head is attached to the end of a flat metal rod affixed to a spring at the back of the figure.

If this is not to be your opening trick, keep the figure covered with a large cloth. Otherwise, Freddy will distract attention while the earlier feats are performed.

The inflated balloon that replaces the lost head is fastened to the front of the figure just below the top. The neck of the balloon goes between two protruding nail heads; then the rubber is stretched over the nail heads.

Draw the boy's features on the balloon with a wide-tipped felt marking pen, supporting the back of the balloon with your free hand.

As the magic word is shouted, release the catch. The needle extending from the nose of the concealed head breaks the balloon as the head pops into place.

If you use a cutout figure of a small girl, you will find that Forgetful Felicia is just as appealing to children as Freddy, her older brother.

A yellow or orange balloon obviously is better than one of dark blue or purple. Black marks on the latter colors are scarcely visible from a distance.

Be sure that the head springs up with sufficient force for the needle to puncture the balloon.

SANTA'S SUIT

Party magicians are busier during the Christmas season than at any other time of the year. Many of the performances are for children. Tricks with a Yuletide plot have a strong appeal. This one dramatizes a North Pole dilemma.

Displaying a twenty-four-inch-tall Santa Claus, the magician says he will explain why the bearded, rose-cheeked figure is wearing old-fashioned winter underwear instead of the traditional fur-trimmed red velvet suit.

"When Santa hopped out of bed on Christmas Eve to prepare for his seasonal journey," the magician continues, "his clothes were missing. Neither he nor his elves could find them. Perhaps, Santa thought, they had been packed by mistake in one of the sacks filled with candy canes and toys. He didn't mind streaking through the air in his sled clad only in underwear, but he knew that millions of children would be disappointed. If they glimpsed him, they might think he was a bewhiskered hippy out on a lark. It was too late to alert the FBI or Scotland Yard. Besides, he doubted their authority extended to the polar regions. So he tried to make a long-distance telephone call to me. Each time Santa dialed he received a busy signal.

Sometimes the reactions of youngsters are funnier than anything a magician can say or do. The perplexed boy indicates his amazement.

"Finally an operator answered. Santa told her who he was, but at first she didn't believe him. 'Fourteen people have already claimed to be Santa Claus tonight,' she said, 'Who are you trying to call? The Easter Bunny? If you're really Santa Claus, give me a merry ho, ho, ho.'" He did. She was convinced, and she put the call through.

"How many of you have ever talked with Santa Claus?" the magician asks. "Wave your hands." The children who think they have spoken to Santa seated on a golden throne in a department-store toy shop, or ringing a bell on a downtown street corner indicate the fact. Those who suspect that Santa Claus is their father smile knowingly.

"This is how I solved Santa's problem," the magician says. He covers the figure with an oblong wooden tube. The underwear is hidden but the head and booted feet can be seen. Taking a tiny fur-trimmed red hat from a black cloth bag, the magician puts the hat on Santa's head. Digging deeper in the bag, he finds the missing red suit. Replacing the jacket and the pants in the bag, he asks the children to call out the magic words, "Merry Christmas." He acknowledges this greeting with, "And a Merry Christmas to you." The bag is turned inside out. It is empty.

When the cover that concealed Santa's body is lifted, the bearded man is fully clothed.

The bottom of the painted plywood Santa Claus fits snugly in a slot in the wooden base. The white-trimmed red suit is glued to the body. A piece of metal extending from the whiskers to the tops of the painted boots is covered with white cloth to simulate long underwear on the front and painted black at the back. It is held on the figure by wire tabs at the shoulders and at the center.

Three Alnico magnets are embedded in the flat wooden tube on the inner side of the front panel. The tube is painted black. The tube should be wide enough to fit easily over Santa and his hat. When the back of the front panel touches the "underwear," the metal to which the cloth is glued will cause the "underwear" to adhere to the magnets in the tube.

The ten- by twelve-inch cloth bag into which Santa's suit disappears is divided into two sections by a partition made of the same black material as the bag. With the suit in one pocket, the other is turned inside out to make it appear that the bag is empty.

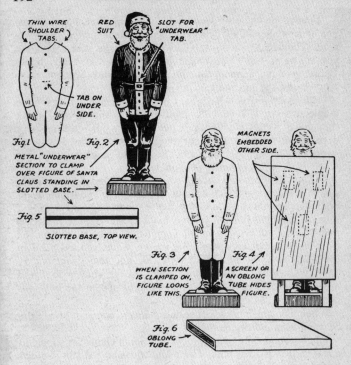

THIN WIRE SHOULDER TABS.

RED SUIT

SLOT FOR "UNDERWEAR" TAB.

TAB ON UNDER SIDE.

Fig.1   *Fig.2*

METAL "UNDERWEAR" SECTION TO CLAMP OVER FIGURE OF SANTA CLAUS STANDING IN SLOTTED BASE.

Fig.5

SLOTTED BASE, TOP VIEW.

MAGNETS EMBEDDED OTHER SIDE.

Fig.3   *Fig.4*

WHEN SECTION IS CLAMPED ON, FIGURE LOOKS LIKE THIS.

A SCREEN OR AN OBLONG TUBE HIDES FIGURE.

Fig.6
OBLONG TUBE.

As the cover is lifted from Santa, the "underwear," held to the inner side of the oblong tube by the magnets, comes away with it.

POPSICLE

Between tricks, the magician takes from his pocket a bar of chocolate-covered ice cream on a stick, removes the paper wrapper, and raises the confection to his lips. He stops just before he tastes it, looks at it hard, then says, "I wonder why they called these things Popsicles?" A sudden exploding noise startles him. He says, "Now, I know," then puts the ice cream into his pocket.

The wrapper is real, but the bar of chocolate-covered ice

Even the pigeons of Trafalgar Square, London, were startled when Milbourne Christopher suddenly produced a live rabbit from nowhere.

cream is made of wood. Properly painted, it looks exactly like the genuine article, with one exception. Embedded at the back is a shooting device, one of the oblong metal noise-makers sold in novelty shops. When the cover is released, a spring sends a striking panel agains a cap—the sort used in toy pistols—and the cap explodes.

As the paper wrapper covers the imitation Popsicle, it may be shown freely until the wrapper is lifted off. When the popping sound comes from the ice cream, look surprised, then put the Popsicle back in your pocket.

Don't be startled when after the show youngsters ask you if the ice cream melted in your pocket.

Miscellaneous Magic

Not infrequently impromptu feats are more astonishing than those presented in shows. In Rio de Janeiro, Havana, and Honolulu I have heard people who saw Max Malini's fountain-pen suspension tell of the amazement this casual bit of conjuring produced.

Malini would touch a pen with his fingers, and the pen would adhere. Though he shook his hand, the pen would not fall but stayed there—until he commanded it to drop.

THE FLOATING PEN

The magician touches the tips of his right-hand fingers to a ball-point pen, which rests on the open fingers of his left hand. Nothing happens. He briskly rubs his fingertips on the sleeve of his coat, then tries again. This time the pen adheres. He lifts his hand; then turning it in various directions, he shakes his hand. Still the pen stays firm.

Holding his right palm toward the audience, the magician slowly spreads his fingers. Still the pen adheres. He brings his fingers together, then touches the pen to the fingertips of his left hand. It sticks to them. He transfers the pen from one hand to the other, back and forth, without dropping it.

Finally he puts the pen on the extended fingers of his left hand, then drapes a handkerchief over it. Again rubbing his right-hand fingers briskly on his sleeve, he touches them to the covered pen. When he lifts them, the pen comes up with them. Though he transfers the covered pen from one hand to another, it does not fall.

The pen and the handkerchief can be examined thoroughly both before and after the suspension.

The gimmick is made from a small disk of metal, bent to snap on to the curvature of a pen. Fastened securely to the center of the disk is a small headless nail, as shown in the illustration. The gimmick is painted black to match the pen.

The pen with the gimmick snapped in place, as depicted in the second drawing, is carried in your inside coat pocket. A white handkerchief is worn in your breast pocket.

Take the pen from your pocket, display it on the open fingers of your left hand. The nail is on the lower side of the pen between the index and middle fingers.

After generating "static electricity" by rubbing your right fingertips on your left sleeve, touch the fingers to the top of the pen. Roll the pen forward. This will cause the pen to revolve, and the nail will come up between the index and middle fingers. Hold your fingers tightly together.

When you lift your right hand, the pen will rise, too. The right hand may now be turned, and the pen will not fall, if you continue to grip the nail between your fingers.

Holding the palm of your hand toward your audience, open your fingers slowly. The fifth drawing shows how this is done. The nail of the gimmick is balanced on the middle finger. Then bring your fingers together. This is a very deceptive move.

Once more gripping the nail firmly between the index and middle fingers, bring your hands together, palm to palm and fingers to fingers. Roll the pen with the pressure of your left-hand fingers. The nail of the gimmick will revolve so you can grip it between your left index and middle fingers.

Take your right hand away. Apparently, the "magnetism" has been transferred to your left fingers. The pen clings to them.

When the right-hand fingers touch the pen again, they roll it forward and the nail can be gripped again by the right fingers.

Eventually close your right hand around the pen and snap off the gimmick, Put the pen on your open left hand, then cover it

Fig. 1

CLIP-ON GIMMICK SHOWING NAIL GRIP.

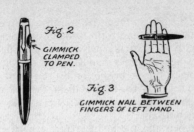

Fig. 2

GIMMICK CLAMPED TO PEN.

Fig. 3

GIMMICK NAIL BETWEEN FINGERS OF LEFT HAND.

Fig. 4

NAIL

RIGHT FINGER TIPS ON PEN, ROLL IT FORWARD TO BRING THE NAIL AROUND.

Fig. 5

FINGERS OPEN WIDE. GIMMICK NAIL IS NOW BALANCED ON MIDDLE FINGER.

Fig 6

GIMMICK CLAMPED OUTSIDE ON COVERED PEN

NAIL

Fig. 7

FINGERS COVER GIMMICK WHEN HAND IS SLANTED.

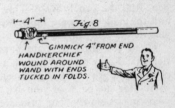

Fig. 8

←4"→

GIMMICK 4" FROM END

HANDKERCHIEF WOUND AROUND WAND WITH ENDS TUCKED IN FOLDS.

with the handkerchief that, until now, has stayed in the breast pocket of your coat.

To make the covered pen adhere to your right-hand fingers, press the gimmick back in position as your right hand touches the handkerchief.

The slightly bent fingers of your hand conceal the gimmick as the pen floats up. The seventh illustration shows the position of the fingers.

Following the covered suspension, the right hand pulls away the handkerchief, and with it the gimmick. The hidden gimmick goes with the handkerchief into your breast pocket. Should someone wish to examine the handkerchief, remove it, but leave the gimmick behind.

THE SUSPENDED WAND

As you may have suspected, on occasion I present the Floating Pen routine with a wand. Before the performance, the gimmick is clipped onto the wand four inches in from one end. A silk handkerchief, held diagonally, is also wound tightly around this end, with the outer corner tucked into a fold, so the handkerchief will not expand prematurely. The eighth drawing shows the positions of the handkerchief and gimmick.

When I remove the wand from inside my coat, my closed right hand hides both the gimmick and the silk.

I touch the unprepared end of the wand to the palm of my left hand to indicate that the hand is empty. Closing this hand around the wand, then sliding my hand down, I turn the upper end of the wand to the right. This swings the lower, prepared end into my left hand. Holding the wrapped handkerchief firmly with my left ring and little fingers, I tap the free end of the wand on my right-hand palm. The right hand then closes on the wand just above my left fist and removes the wand, leaving the handkerchief in my left hand.

A tap of the wand on the back of my closed left hand produces the silk. I rub the silk on the wand to generate "static electricity." Later, I drape the silk over the wand for the final floating sequence. This routine is effective from any angle and may be shown with an audience seated on every side, as well as performed on a stage; that is, it can be if one part is omitted —displaying the wand with the fingers open.

TAPED MAGIC LESSON

"Home-study instructions are now available on cassettes for karate, chess, and conjuring. I received this one in the mail this morning," the magician says as he fits a cassette into a portable tape machine and presses the "Play" lever.

"Today you'll learn how to do the incredible Indonesian silk illusion," the recorded voice begins. "With it you'll earn hundreds, thousands—of compliments from your friends. Reach in your right-hand trouser pocket and take out the yellow silk handkerchief."

The magician puts his hand in his left pocket.

"Your *right* pocket," the voice commands.

As the handkerchief is being withdrawn from the right-hand pocket, the voice instructs, "Toss it in the air and catch it." When this has been done, the voice remarks, "That's probably the most strenuous exercise you've had this week. Tuck one corner of the yellow silk into your left fist, push the silk the rest of the way in; then, as the music plays, pull it out from the far side."

The yellow changes to red as the handkerchief passes through the fist. The music stops, and the taped voice says, "Next week —the vanishing martini."

"What about the red silk in my fist?" the magician asks.

"The vanishing martini," the voice continues, "can be shown with the sleeves rolled up to the elbows."

"The red silk," the magician pleads.

"The vanishing martini is a pleasing deception for the cocktail hour. What's that? The red silk? Simply wiggle the fingers of your right hand, then open your left fingers."

The magician follows these instructions. He opens his fingers, his left hand is empty. The sound of a large audience applauding comes from the tape machine.

A metal tube measuring 2 inches in length and ¾ inch in diameter, is loaded with a red silk handkerchief and placed in the left trousers pocket before the start of the routine. To load the silk, fold back one corner two inches, then pack the handkerchief tightly into the tube. The diagonal corner is also folded back at the far end.

When, seemingly by mistake, the magician puts his left hand into his left trousers pocket, his fingers close around the tube and mask it from view as his hand is withdrawn.

The right-hand index finger pushes the yellow silk into the thumb side of the closed left hand. After each push, the right hand reaches across and pulls more of the red from the far side of the fist. When the red silk is free of the tube, the left little finger retains it as the right index finger, inserted in the opposite end of the tube, bends around the left thumb to bring the tube into the right hand.

Once the tube is concealed there, the right hand pulls the yellow silk from the far side of the left fist and puts it—and the tube—into the right trousers pocket.

Illusionist John Daniel offered a new conjuring concept in this kitchen magic scene from his night-club revue. Pots and ovens replaced cabinets.

The left fist remains closed until the recorded voice tells the magician to open it.

You may prefer to have the recorded voice tell you how to do a card trick or a feat of mentalism. Before portable tape machines were available, I used a record and a record player in theatres and night-clubs. Now, with miniature tape machines, the unseen instructor can give his instructions almost anywhere.

A CHOICE OF CASSETTES

When cassettes replaced reels in smaller tape machines, I devised this feat. Eight cassettes were shown. I inserted them one by one in a machine and played just enough from each so that the varying styles of music could be identified. They were a violin solo, Dixieland jazz, a Sinatra ballad, an aria from an opera, a rumba, a spiritual, a plaintive folk song, and a Sousa march. The cassettes were not labeled. I told a volunteer to mix the cassettes, then put them into a large paper bag. This same person held the bag as another volunteer reached in and chose a cassette.

My head was turned away as the choice was being made. I wrote a prediction on a large pad, concealing the writing until after the chosen cassette had been inserted in the machine by the person who selected it and the music played. Invariably the prediction was accurate.

All but one of the cassettes were prepared in this way: Seven began with ten seconds of another style of music then switched abruptly to a Sousa march; the eighth cassette was a Sousa march from start to finish.

I played precisely ten seconds of each tape to convey the idea that eight choices were possible. No matter which cassette was chosen later, I knew that martial music would be heard when the cassette was in the machine.

VANISHING SMOKE

Ted Bohmann presented an unusual routine when I visited his Magic Lounge in Milwaukee several years ago. Removing a Coca-Cola bottle from behind the bar, he filled it with cigar smoke, puffed through a soda straw.

He asked onlookers to estimate how long it would take him to remove the smoke from the bottle. There were several answers; none correct. He struck a match, dropped it into the bottle; there was a flash—and the smoke gushed out instantly.

Though the bottle appeared to be empty when the trick was shown, there was a small amount of Scotch whisky in it. The lighted match set off a small-scale explosion, immediately forcing out the smoke.

As a soda bottle, rather than one that had contained alcohol, was used, spectators had no clue to the mystery.

DWINDLING SMOKE

Bohmann followed the first smoke feat with another that had an unexpected finish. Once more, he puffed cigar smoke through a straw into the bottle, then lit a match. He didn't drop this lighted match down the neck of the bottle; instead he held the flame to the opening. The smoke slowly curled *downward,* then disappeared.

A few drops of whisky remained in the bottle after the previous trick. While attention was elsewhere, he pressed his thumb over the mouth of the bottle, turned the bottle upside down and shook it to coat the inner walls. Then he put the bottle right side up on the bar, and was ready for the second phase of the exhibition. When the flame was put to the mouth of the bottle, it touched the invisible liquid coating and the reaction already described occurred.

Hoping to strengthen the impact of these smoke tricks, the magician-barman experimented for several weeks. He found that a solution made by mixing two ounces of whisky with one of 90-proof white crème de cacao would work better than straight whisky. A transparent beer bottle with sides that tapered from a wide bottom to a narrow top was more effective for his purpose than the curved Cola bottle he had previously employed. He kept several of these empty beer bottles, which had been thoroughly washed, within easy reach at the back of the bar. Near to them was a stoppered bottle with the whisky-crème de cacao solution.

Before beginning the smoke routine, Bohmann secretly poured several drops of the mixture into one of the empty bottles; then he put this bottle on the bar.

Three puffs of cigar smoke, blown through a straw, were enough to fill the bottle. When the lighted match fell in the bottle, the smoke disappeared.

He varied the handling of the second trick. After puffing smoke into the bottle, he openly turned the bottle upside down to shake out the burned match and coat the sides with the residue of the solution. Turning the bottle upright, he applied the second burning match to the mouth, and was pleased to see that the slanting sides enhanced the sinking and evaporating smoke presentation.

The combination of the two feats, with the second immediately following the first, and with a logical reason for shaking the inverted bottle was a great improvement.

When the tricks are performed in a room with subdued lighting, the eerie action of the smoke is quite intriguing.

SENSITIVE NEWSPRINT

British magician Paul Graham saw a curious trick at the Wheatsheaf Inn in Old Oxted, Surrey. He told me about it in my dressing room at the Brighton Hippodrome. Graham said a stranger standing near him at the bar casually ripped a strip from a London newspaper, then folded it lengthwise. Holding the strip upright between his left thumb and fingers, the man struck a match with his right hand and brought it close to the paper. The top of the strip slowly bent as though attracted by the flame. Before the paper could ignite, the stranger raised the match, and the strip straightened. Then he set the paper afire and used it to light a cigarette.

The man, whose name Graham did not know, taught him how to do the stunt.

You can prepare for this trick in a few seconds. Starting at the lower left side of the back page of a newspaper, make an upward 2-inch tear, ¾ inch in from and parallel to the left edge.

When performing, rip away a strip 7 inches long and 1½ inches wide from the lower left corner of the page. Fold this in half length-wise. The fold hides the short tear previously made as the paper is creased along and above the tear.

Grasp the folded strip between your left thumb and index finger with the ball of the thumb ⅛ inch below the top of the secret tear.

A slight downward pressure by the thumb will pull the paper it touches and force the strip to bend. Push your thumb up, and the strip will straighten.

Paul Graham said that the man in the pub dropped the flaming strip into an ashtray after he lit his cigarette, thus destroying the paper and any evidence that the strip had been prepared.

Chinese actress Tisa Chang sits on thin air after Christopher removes the hassock on which she had been perched, during his opening feat.

This is a most unusual close-up trick. Don't turn the page without trying it.

The bending strip can be used as a dowsing rod to point to a previously chosen card—if you know the position of the card in the face-up pack.

When performing for children use a pen or a pencil instead of a match to motivate the paper. Otherwise, some youngster may set his house ablaze as he tries to duplicate the trick.

DOWSING STICKS

For centuries dowsers have tried to locate subterranean water or silver mines with pendulums or forked twigs. In recent years L-shaped metal rods have been more used than in the past for this purpose.

I met an American engineer aboard an ocean liner bound for Brazil who carried a pair of divining rods in a leather case in his inside coat pocket. The bent sticks were eight inches long with three-inch handles. They were made of silver. Holding the rods loosely with his fingers curled around the handles and the long ends extending forward over the sides of his index fingers, he demonstrated his skill. His hands were eight inches apart, and the horizontal ends were parallel.

After touching the tips of the sticks to the green paint of the ship's rail, he walked away, then came back. When the rods were directly above the rail, they mysteriously crossed to form an X.

With his permission, I tried to duplicate the experiment—and succeeded. My eyes had been on his hands, not on the tips of the rods. I saw that his fists had turned inwardly very, very slightly when the rods were above the rail. This caused the ends to swing together and cross.

I am sure he was not aware of this almost imperceptible movement. Knowing how the rods had been activated, it was easy for me to duplicate his actions.

Since then I have frequently used similar dowsing sticks during my performances. Some I have cut and shaped from metal coat hangers. Others I have made from half inch in diameter aluminum tubing. The latter are more visible on a stage. The extending sections are twelve inches long; the handles measure four inches from tip to L-shaped bend.

I can cause the rods to cross simply by visualizing the action. My hands follow the directions of my brain. That is, I do not move them consciously.

I do not claim to be a dowser, I demonstrate what happens when dowsers are at work. For example, I touch the tips of the rods to a woman's red pocketbook. Then I hold the rods over other colors, and they remain motionless. A red scarf, dress, or necklace will cause them to swing together and overlap. Or I touch the rods to a silver coin, and they will be set in motion by the silver objects spectators display, but not by copper or aluminum.

Audiences enjoy these dowsing feats. When I say I do not have occult powers, some people do not believe me.

FRIENDLY SPIRITS

Poltergeists thump on walls in the dead of the night, hurl objects across rooms, and smash crockery. Poltergeists, in most reported cases, manifest themselves in homes where small children live. The unseen forces that aid the magician in this presentation are of a less destructive nature.

Resting on a tray held by an assistant is an oblong box. Draw curtains are at the front and back of the box. When they are opened, the audience can see through the box. When they are closed, the manifestations occur. Placing a dinner bell in the box, then closing the curtains, the magician says, "If friendly spirits are here, they'll make their presence known." Immediately the bell starts ringing.

Assuming the spirits are in an amiable mood, the magician tells the audience that the bell will answer questions. One ring for yes, two for no. Should the bell ring three times, the spirits are hedging with "perhaps."

Queries are posed, and the bell sounds in each instance. Then a blank slate and a piece of chalk take the place of the bell behind the drapes. Conditions are right, the magician assures the spectators, for a ghostly message. Usually this is a prediction or a warning. The message duly appears on the slate.

Next a flashlight is put in the cabinet and the stage lights are lowered. A light flashes on behind the curtains and moves back and forth. It fades away. There are three ominous knocks, and a small luminous ghost peeks through the drapes. As music plays, the ghost dances up and down, then darts away. The stage lights go up. The curtains are opened. There is no trace of the ghost. The magician quickly takes the box apart, then piles the pieces on the tray. Nothing is seen that could account for the manifestations.

The assistant carries the tray offstage. The moment he disappears in the wings, there is a terrific clatter, the sound of breaking glass, and falling objects.

"The spirits," the magician explains, "are not quite as friendly as I thought."

The young woman in the Egyptian sarcophagus will be sliced into three pieces by Christopher, then the center portion will disappear.

The box itself is unprepared. The top, bottom, and sides are made of wood. The pieces are fastened together with dowels, so that the box can be taken apart quickly.

The secret of the séance lies in the assistant's third hand. Two hold the sides of the tray. One, however, is not real. It is at the end of a false arm, strapped to his body, as shown in the illustration. The second real hand is concealed by the costume. It is the second hand that reaches into the box from the back,

CURTAINS AT BACK AND FRONT.

ASSISTANT HOLDING TRAY AND CABINET.

Fig. 1

POSITION OF REAL ARM UNDER COAT.

FLOWERS AND GHOST.

FAKE ARM

FAKE ARM AND PLASTIC HAND.

Fig. 2

VIEW WITH CABINET OMITTED.

SHOWING HOW RIGHT HAND COMES OUT OF COAT TO RING BELL.

Fig. 3

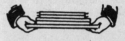

CABINET IS BROKEN DOWN AT FINISH. DOWELS AT TOP AND BOTTOM OF SIDES, FIT INTO HOLES IN THE TOP AND BOTTOM SECTIONS TO HOLD CABINET TOGETHER.

Fig. 4

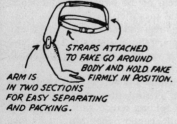

STRAPS ATTACHED TO FAKE GO AROUND BODY AND HOLD FAKE FIRMLY IN POSITION.

ARM IS IN TWO SECTIONS FOR EASY SEPARATING AND PACKING.

Fig. 5

FAKE HAND IS FASTENED BY A BOLT TO THE TRAY.

Fig. 6

rings the bell, writes on the slate, turns the flashlight on and off, produces the three raps and the luminous cloth that masquerades as a ghost.

The presentation must be thoroughly rehearsed. The assistant's work is not difficult, but it must be perfectly timed. You can, if you wish, vary the mysterious manifestations. Fresh flowers can appear—if the assistant has them concealed within easy reach on his body.

Don't let the routine become overlong. Three questions are enough for the spirits to answer. One or two words on the slate are as mystifying as twenty. The prediction can be for the next day's weather—fair, cloudy; cold, hot; clear, rain, or snow. Remember, the alleged spirits are giving this information. They are notoriously poor prophets. Yet I have found that the predictions written on the slate are as accurate as those you read in the newspaper, or hear on radio and television.

The luminous cloth has been saturated with Strobelite, a reliable material supplied by the firm of that name in New York City. The flashlight serves two purposes. It produces an eerie effect as it seems to float behind the curtains and it shines on the luminous cloth, which otherwise would not be nearly so visible when it appears.

QUICK-CHANGE ILLUSION

The magician begins his show dressed in Oriental robes, a Chinese cap, and wearing a Fu Manchu beard and spectacles. After a few quick tricks, he goes behind a screen with a windowlike opening in the center panel, and pulls down a shade. Immediately the stage lights are lowered, and an assistant switches on a spotlight at the rear of the screen. The audience sees the shadow of the Oriental mystifier on the shade. Suddenly the shade flies up. The magician has made an instant change of costume. He now appears in a dinner jacket or tailcoat, the Chinese trappings have vanished along with the facial adornments.

The performer steps from behind the screen and continues the show as himself rather than as a mystifier from the Orient.

You will need a three-panel folding screen with an opening, as shown in the illustration, in the center panel. Mounted above the window, on the side away from the audience, is a white window shade coated with Strobelite. Behind the screen is a spotlight with a color wheel. If the performer works alone, he turns this light on and off by a switch on the floor operated by his foot.

When the magician in Chinese attire strides behind the screen, he pulls down the shade and steps on the switch. White light from the spotlight floods the screen. His sharply defined shadow is seen from the front. He raises his arms, then treads on the switch. It seems that a green light is projected from the back. Actually the spot is off. The green is the luminous material around the shadow that was produced earlier. Working at lightning speed, the magician strips off the costume and disguise. He extends his hands, and takes a position similar to that on the screen. The white spot goes on and blots out the earlier green. He touches the shade release with his foot, and the blind shoots up to reveal the rapid change. He walks to the front of the stage as the curtains close behind him, so that stagehands can remove the screen, spot, and other material.

FEMALE TO MALE

The lighting change may be employed in many ways. For example, a woman walks behind the screen and is instantly converted into a man, if the man is crouching down so that he cannot be seen through the opening, and if the woman hides in the same way after he takes her place while the green "light" is on.

PICTURE TO LIFE

Most large-scale stage feats call for an outlay of several thousand dollars. This illusion can be produced with a minimum of expense.

Standing in front of a pair of overlapping stage curtains, the magician dons an artist's smock, a wig, a beard, and a beret. He goes through the curtains, which open immediately to reveal the full stage, and walks to a table. He picks up a palette and several brushes as an assistant wheels a "canvas," six feet high by three feet wide, to the center of the stage. The magician-

Seconds before Christopher's full-grown elephant vanished on CBS-TV World's Greatest Magicians hour of fabricated amazement.

artist quickly sketches the outline of a man wearing a cape and a high silk hat. Suddenly a cane breaks through the "canvas." The painter flees into the wings, and a man steps through the "canvas." It is the magician who only a second before had darted from view.

A double is used in this illusion. The double is dressed in a smock, beret, beard, and wig that matches those worn by the magician.

The moment the magician, dressed as an artist, goes through the overlapping front curtains, the double, with his back to the audience, walks from the curtains to the table. Remember, the curtains open just after the magician passes through them.

The magician meanwhile has darted to the wings, ripped off his painter's costume and disguise, put on a top hat and a cape, and stepped to the back of the "canvas" that the assistant pushes from the wings to center stage.

The "canvas" is paper, tacked to the back of an oblong frame on a base equipped with rollers. After the double draws the outline on the paper, the concealed magician takes a cane from a clip at the back of the frame, then thrusts it through the paper.

Fig. 1

PERFORMER, IN CHINESE COSTUME, WALKS BEHIND SCREEN AND PULLS DOWN SHADE.

Fig. 2

HIS SHADOW IS SEEN. THEN INSTANTLY THE SHADE FLIES UP.

Fig. 3

THE PERFORMER IS NOW SEEN IN MODERN CLOTHES.

STROBELITE WINDOW BLIND

CATCH TO HOLD SHADE DOWN

FOOT RELEASE FOR SHADE

FOOT CONTROL FOR SPOTLIGHT WITH COLOR WHEEL

Fig. 4

The double dashes offstage. The magician breaks the paper and steps forward.

Tiny slits in the paper running like small dotted lines from the diagonal corners and crossing at the center will make it easier for the magician to break through the paper. Similar slits at the point he will jab with the sharpened end of the cane will aid in this impalement.

THE MARTIAN MYSTERY

The front-curtain switch may be used in various other ways. A woman assistant, dressed as an astronaut and wearing a helmet, goes through the curtains. The curtains open as she walks toward an upright box. When she steps inside, the front panel of the box is closed. The magician fires a pistol. The front of the box starts to open, then stops. The woman astronaut runs down the aisle to the front of the theatre. When she mounts the steps to the stage, the door of the box swings wide, and a weird green creature, obviously from Outer Space, leaps out.

The double, whose face is painted green and who wears a green costume under the astronaut garb and helmet, takes the place of the woman astronaut as she seemingly goes through the curtains and into the box. As only the back of the double is seen, the green makeup is concealed.

The astronaut runs around the theatre to the front of the house, then sprints down the aisle. To give her time to do so, several things have been occurring on stage. The magician switches on several lights at the sides of the box, looks up, then signals his assistants to move the box more to the right. If the box has been painted to resemble a rocket, this will strengthen the impact of the illusion.

Meanwhile the double has stripped away the outer garb and removed the helmet, allowing the antenna on her Martian headpiece to extend. There should be a blackout a moment after the Martian leaps from the box—and a scream from the woman astronaut.

The crucial moment in any of the various curtain-switch presentations is the one when one person goes through the curtains and the second person creates the impression that the same person has continued walking. Properly rehearsed, with an alert stagehand opening the curtains, the change will not be detected.

The shoes of the double must be identical to those worn by the performer whose place is taken. As a boy, I saw a magician's double with brown shoes stand in a cabinet though the man he impersonated wore black patent-leather pumps.

The double, of course, should also be the same height as the performer. I remember another show in which a girl disappeared from one box and emerged six inches shorter from another.

A pair of identical twins with the Thurston production never left the stage door together, and, though they were blonde, one wore a brunette wig when she was away from the footlights.

TWENTIETH-CENTURY SAWING

During one of the last evenings I spent with Jean Hugard, he reminisced about the illusions he had presented as a young man in Australia. One I had never seen: A sword placed point upward under a floating woman pierced through her body when she descended. Remaining briefly in place on the blade, she then soared up once more and soon afterward took her bow, unmarked and unharmed.

We talked of Sawing a Woman in Half, the biggest box-office illusion attraction in vaudeville, and of the many methods that had been devised to create this effect. I sketched out still another way to present the illusion. Later Abril Lamarque made the drawings that accompany this description.

Basically a buzz saw severs the body of a woman as she rests horizontally on a thin board; then it slices through the board. Two young women are concealed in the apparatus. (The illustration shows the positions they occupy.) The pillars, which support the board, and the base are hinged at the back to permit easy entry and exit.

Only the first girl's head is in view. A realistic fake body extends from her neck to the knees of the second girl, whose feet are seen.

The first girl closes her eyes before the buzz saw reaches the body. The second girl moves her feet slightly as the blade saws, but this action should not be emphasized.

The equipment is preset behind the front curtains before the presentation begins. The second girl is in position. The illusionist puts on a surgical gown and cap while standing in front of the closed curtains. As he does so, his personality changes. Acting the role of a mad doctor, he calls for his minions to strap the girl who helped him to don the costume to a torture board. She runs screaming from the stage. Noticing another possible victim in the front row, the mad doctor starts down the steps. A scream from behind the curtains makes him change his mind. He returns to the stage, and the curtains open. The assistant is strapped to the board; the buzz saw revolves. The mad doctor

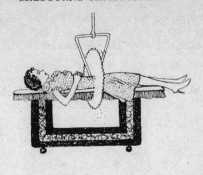

guides the saw through the body—and the board. After the operation, the curtains close. The illusionist strides forward. When he removes the white cap and robe, he is himself again.

"I'm sure you realize," he says, "that what you saw was just an illusion. It was a very realistic illusion, however. The young lady unfortunately will not be able to take a bow."

A magician with a full-length show can conceal the base of the apparatus in a large platform, rising fourteen inches above the stage.

The illusion can be shown in a circus with the audience seated on every side. In that case the girl, strapped to the board, would be wheeled into the center ring.

When two cuts have been made through the body—the second one twelve inches from the first—the center section of the body can be lifted out, then replaced.

THE INVISIBLE MAGICIAN

The most amazing illusion shown at the 1952 convention of the Society of American Magicians in Boston was not performed on a stage. It was presented in a dealer-display room by Ken Allen, an ingenious manufacturer of conjuring equipment from New Jersey.

Two friends held up a blanket to hide the slender young man from view. When they dropped the blanket, he was gone. Spectators were invited to search every closet, box, and corner of the display room and the adjacent bathroom. There were no windows. A single door led to the area from a corridor. It was locked before the demonstration began. It could also have been bolted or sealed for it was on the spectator side of the blanket. John Dickson Carr and Clayton Rawson, specialists in locked-room detective mysteries, would have been puzzled by this disappearance. It astonished such celebrated deceptionists as Long Tack Sam, John Booth, and Al Delage.

When the searchers admitted they had probed every possible hiding place, Allen's friends held up the blanket again. They let it fall, and Ken stepped over it to acknowledge the applause.

There was something very peculiar about the display area that Allen had discovered by chance when he was trying to open a bottle of beer. The opener was fastened to a small cabinet above the washstand in the bathroom. The bottle cap did not budge. Ken yanked on the bottle and pulled the cabinet away from the wall. The right side was hinged to a frame in an oblong hole. The hinges could not be seen from the bathroom. Ken put his head through the opening and saw a square air shaft that extended floors below and floors above. The sides were grimy, but it occurred to him, that if he cleaned them, he could perform a feat no one had ever before attempted. He worked most of the night scouring the soot from the sides of the shaft. The next day he put on tennis shoes, crawled through the hole, braced himself with the rubber soles on the far side, and devised a fastening device, so that if a curious magician yanked on the cabinet as he had, it would not come open.

Then, with the help of two friends, he sped from behind an improvised cover—a hotel blanket—and into his hiding place. They timed how long it took him to conceal himself and how many seconds elapsed during the reentry maneuver.

The feat, when shown, was flawlessly executed. Repetition several times each day did not lessen the mystery.

I don't advise readers to gamble with fate as Allen did each time he entered the air shaft, but I hope they will take advantage of circumstances as quickly as he did and devise new approaches to conjuring of their own.

Christopher conjures during a skit in front of a police roadblock on the CBS-TV Comedy Hour in 1970.